1975

# Anthropology

# Anthropology:
## THE HUMANIZING PROCESS

### EVELYN S. KESSLER
University of South Florida

### Allyn and Bacon, Inc.
### Boston

Library of Congress Catalog Card Number: 73-92029.

# Contents

Preface    ix

1. IT'S ONLY A THEORY    1
   Concepts of Science
   Can We Live with Science?

2. WOULD THAT GOD THE GIFTIE GIE US    8
   What Is an Anthropologist?
   What Is Culture?
   Anthropological Method
   Ethnocentrism and Cultural Relativism

3. THE NAKED APE    20
   Natural Selection
   Continuing Evolution
   Cultural Selection
   History of Fossil Man
   Australopithecus
   Homo Erectus
   Neanderthal Man
   Modern Man

v

4. HE LOOKS JUST LIKE UNCLE JOE    36
   *Baboons*
   *Chimpanzees*
   *Chimpanzee Communication*

5. WHAT COLOR ARE COLORED PEOPLE?    48
   *Defining Race*
   *The Biology of Race*
   *Racism in America*

6. IN THE WORD WAS THE BEGINNING    61
   *History of Language*
   *Structure of Language*
   *Language Change*
   *Language Symbolism*
   *Written Language*
   *Anthropology and Linguistics*

7. WHY DIG HOLES IN THE GROUND?    70
   *Techniques of the Archaeologist*
   *Artifacts*
   *Remains of Homo Erectus*
   *Remains of Neanderthal Man*
   *Remains of Modern Man*
   *After the Pleistocene*

8. LOST CITIES AND BURIED TREASURE    85
   *Civilization in the Americas*
   *Agriculture*
   *Mesoamerican Civilization*

9. IT's HUMAN NATURE    96
*Instinct versus Learning*
*Violence in Society*
*Warfare*

10. $E = M \times T \times R \times E$    105
*Cultural Development*
*Computing Technological Efficiency*
*Specific Development of Technologies*
*Cultural Subsystems*

11. MONEY ISN'T EVERYTHING    113
*Hunting and Gathering Economies*
*Subsistence Agriculture Economies*
*Stored Wealth Economies*
*Market Economies*

12. WHAT HAS BECOME OF THE FAMILY?    121
*Functions of Marriage*
*Marriage Systems*
*Joint or Extended Families*
*Nuclear Families*
*Kinship*
*Change in American Marriage Patterns*

13. WHAT IS THE WORLD COMING TO?    133
*Stratification of Societies*
*Colonialism*
*Subcultures in the United States*

*The Culture of Poverty*

*The Counter-Culture*


14. WHICH IS THE WITCH?     144

*Belief Systems*

*Religious Personnel*

*Ritual*

*Functions of Religion*

*Myth and Legend*


15. NOW WHAT? WHERE DO WE GO FROM HERE?     153

*Long-Term Trends in Evolution*

*Population Growth and the Ecosystem*

*Trends in the United States*


Suggested Readings     163

*General Anthropology*

*Physical Anthropology*

*Archaeology*

*Linguistics*

*Cultural Anthropology*

*Anthropology in the Modern World*


Bibliography     165

Index     171

# Preface

*Living in a small community can present many challenges to one who has spent most of her life in a megalopolis. Not the least among these is the viewpoint of the local population as expressed in the letters to the editor of the local newspaper.*

*A short time ago, the community where I live was shaken by a school board member's view that the creation myth should be taught in the schools along with evolutionary theory. A university faculty member, expressing his views in a letter to the editor, objected to lumping mythology with scientific theory.*

*Thereupon came the deluge. The columns were full of letters from people from all walks of life. Some were angry at what they saw as a denunciation of religious dogma. Others expressed the view that scientific theory was simply another form of opinion. Most letter-writers felt that man is a special creation, and even if scientific theories can be applied to other animals, they are not valid with respect to man.*

*No one seemed aware of the anthropological concept of man starting out as a small, undistinguished primate, utilizing poorly made stone tools, proceeding through millions of years of hardship, surviving wild beasts, ice ages, and innumerable perils, learning to make and use fire, to domesticate plants and animals, to build towns and cities, to write books, to found belief systems, to use science. No one seemed aware of the heroic nature of the struggle man has undergone to humanize himself. And no one seemed aware that the process is continuing.*

*This epic drama is exciting and is much more expressive of human potential than a tame belief in special creation. Moreover, note the diversity with which man fashions his life so as to reap the greatest potential in his particular environment given his particular history. This is the very stuff of which great tales are told. This is the basic pattern of any television western or soap opera. Man against the world, ever striving to achieve success, however he measures it.*

*This is what anthropology tells us. It is in anthropology that we have the information to detail the remarkable history of man and his culture.*

*This book was designed to reach the interested human, of whatever age, status, or opinion. One does not require a backlog of formal education to profit from reading it. It is dedicated to every one of us, for we all participate in the humanizing process.*

*I am grateful to my students, my colleagues, and my community for making this book valid. I am grateful to my family, especially B. K., for making it possible.*

# CHAPTER 1

# It's Only a Theory

Anthropology is one of the newest social sciences. Man has always exhibited curiosity about his neighbors and has told some pretty tall tales about them. But it was not until the early 1860s that E. B. Tylor was appointed to the first chair of anthropology at Oxford University. At first, anthropology was regarded as a repository for the antique and the exotic. However, through time, anthropology has shown that it has a unique perspective on man and his world. From this perspective, the anthropologist has some important statements to make about ourselves and our time.

In 1861, Thomas Huxley referred to anthropology as "Mr. Tylor's science." Today, anthropologists number in the hundreds and our students in the thousands. Through books, articles, and radio and TV programs, the anthropological point of view is becoming better known. As public awareness grows, questions arise as to how these views were developed and how valid they are compared to other views.

To start, we shall look at the methods and objectives of science as a whole, and then examine anthropology in this context.

In our time, people tend to hold a dualistic attitude toward science. On the one hand, we are grateful for many things that make our lives safer, easier, and more pleasant. We acknowledge the contributions of science in material objects and in such things as improved health, longevity, and reduction of infant mortality. On the other hand, we fear certain scientific innovations as a threat to our way of life. Nuclear bombs, automation, and pollution are examples of these. We tend to believe, somewhat uncritically, that science can cure all ills and solve all problems. At the same time, we hold the notion of the sinister Dr. Frankenstein loosing his monster on the world. Are either of these seemingly incompatible attitudes justified? What is science and how does it affect our lives?

## Concepts of Science

"Science," says Leslie White (1949:3), "is sciencing." Science is a process, a method of doing things. "It is the process of organizing our knowledge in such a way as to command more of the hidden potential in nature" (Bronowski 1965:7).

Science begins with two basic assumptions. One is that the universe is orderly, subject to natural laws. The second is that these laws can be discovered and used by the man who asks the right questions and applies the proper techniques. In this respect, there is similarity between the scientist and the magician, in that both seek control over the forces of nature, and both assume these forces can be controlled. The scientist, however, applies different techniques to his problems than does the magician.

The scientist is neither a mortal deity nor a cold-blooded monster. He is a person who seeks to understand and manipulate nature. As a human being living in a particular society at a given time, he will have access to a particular accumulation of knowledge. He will be interested in problems that arise out of the needs and understanding of his time and place. The scientist uses data. But the compilation of data alone is not what science is all about.

Doing science is as creative as doing art, music, or literature. It takes painstaking collection of data, analysis, and finally a leap of the imagination to overcome some of the boundaries our senses and the assumptions our time places upon our understanding of the world. Ernest Rutherford and Niels Bohr discerned the model of the atom in the workings of the planetary system (Bronowski 1965:14). They made the leap from the largest system we know to the smallest. In the eighteenth century, Linneaus ordered plant and animal species into a classification system that projected an increase in complexity of organisms. The French naturalist Buffon recognized this and stated that it appeared that different species must in some way be related to each other. However, it remained for the genius of Charles Darwin and Alfred Wallace to elucidate the nature and method of that relationship, when they simultaneously proposed the theory of natural selection over a century ago.

The scientist, then, is a person with a creative mind. The nature of his work also lends itself to a development that Bronowski (1965:27) calls the "habit of truth." In his work, the scientist is constantly testing his data against reality—and here lies the base of the misunderstanding which so often occurs between the scientist and the public.

The scientist usually starts with a problem current to his time and place. In thinking about this problem, he sometimes comes up with a hypothesis. He then proceeds to test his hypothesis by methods specific to his particular science. He collects data, analyzes that data, relates his body of data to other such data, and emerges with his hypothesis tested against reality as he knows it. This is now a theory. The scientist is acutely aware of the fact that his instruments and methods may be primitive compared to those that may be developed in the future. He is aware of the limitations of his data. He recognizes that more sophisticated interpretations of this data will emerge with the growth of knowledge. Thus, he labels his tested hypothesis a theory, hoping that future work will refine it. He does this because he, and others who follow him, will be constantly testing the theory against their concept of reality. They may redefine some aspects of the theory, or they may find data that will permit expansion of the theory. Sometimes, although rarely, a great iconoclast with genius will challenge and overturn the theory. When a scientist says, "This is a theory," he is saying, "This is the truth as we know it for now." However, the layman says, "It's only a theory; this is no better than a guess," or "that is a law; science proved it."

Thus, the layman is not prepared for the variations in our perceptions of the universe, and he is ill-prepared, as well, for changes in his own self-concept. Invention and discovery are constantly changing our perceptions of the reality of the universe. In 1300, most Europeans believed the earth was flat. In fact, any attempt then to state otherwise might have left a person open to charges of lunacy or heresy. Yet two hundred years later, most people believed the earth to be round. Are we, then, to doubt the existence of reality? The earth is no less real. What are its real dimensions and shape? We state the truth as we know it now, and call this a theory. In the future, some improvement in techniques may make possible a more accurate rendering of the earth's dimensions. This will be tested against reality, as far as we are able. Maybe our present concepts will change. However, the true dimensions of the earth will not change, nor will the need to keep questioning be invalidated. We must refrain from assuming that answers are absolutes for all time. Science's business is to continue to question, to test and compare.

His constant testing, probing, and questioning breeds in the scientist an independence of mind, which, ideally, leads him to respect the independence of mind of other human beings. The scientist is neither so abstract as to be completely withdrawn from human values, nor is he so tractable as to become the uncritical puppet of whatever dicta are proposed in his time. If the individual scientist is less than this, he is, after all, only human. Public acceptance of a particular theory depends upon several factors. Louis Agassiz, the renowned naturalist, said the public has three reactions to any new theory: first, they think it is impossible; later, they believe it is against religion; and finally, they think it is something they have always known.

For many people, there is real conflict between the statements of science and the beliefs of religion. This is because, although both science and religion recognize the existence of an orderly universe, their systems are based upon entirely different assumptions. The scientist recognizes the existence of natural laws and regards these as susceptible to solution by man. Problems, according to the scientist, need to be stated properly, investigated correctly, and, with time and perseverance, answers will be found. The larger the body of knowledge, the greater will be the sophistication of scientific inquiry and the greater will be man's control of his universe. Religions also recognize the existence of an orderly universe; however, order is imposed by a supernatural authority. There will forever be mysteries man cannot hope to penetrate. Moreover, ultimate control of the universe and all who inhabit it is in the hands of the supernatural, which must be supplicated, appeased, and celebrated in order to obtain benefits.

There is great comfort to be derived from the assumption that some greater power is in charge of one's well-being, who can be persuaded to guard and reward the faithful. This is particularly true if one believes that man is a special creation and occupies a privileged niche in the universe. It is much more difficult to face the world alone, a frail human being striving to adapt to an indifferent universe. Yet there is an element of heroism in the ongoing struggle of mankind to master his world.

### Can We Live with Science?

Whether observed from the viewpont of religion or science, man is indeed an unusual creature. And he tends to resent any scientific notion which deprecates his self-concept.

White (1949:70–71) suggests that those sciences which touch the human being indirectly are easier for him to accept than those which seem to threaten his individuality or call into question his self-esteem. White points to the fact that data from astronomy, chemistry, or physics find a more ready acceptance than do data from anthropology or psychology. This would appear to hold true in recent times. In 1972, for example, when newspaper headlines proclaimed that physicists had created life in the laboratory, little notice seemed to be taken by the public. But, in the same year, the California school system was besieged by citizens who demanded that the Biblical creation story be given equal emphasis with evolutionary theory in textbooks. However, it was not always true that astronomy, for example, had easy acceptance. Galileo, for instance, was forced to recant his belief that he had proven Copernicus's theory that the sun was the center of the universe. This theory does not seem central to the self-concept of man. During Galileo's time, however, church-held dogma was that man was a special creation of God and that the earth was given to man as his realm. According to that theology, the sun and all the planets revolved about the earth, which was only fitting for God's special creation. Galileo challenged man's concept of himself as the center of the universe, his *anthropocentrism*. To this day, as we shall see, modern man has not outgrown tribal concepts of himself and of his group's special position as compared to other groups.

Each bit of knowledge, no matter how irrelevent it now seems to the self-concept of man, has had to fight for acceptance. More ready acceptance can be won for theories based on controlled laboratory experiments which can be replicated and demonstrated. However, not all science can be done under controlled laboratory conditions. In the social sciences, in particular, controlled conditions cause marked distortions of the entities being observed. Early studies of baboons and chimpanzees living in zoos, for example, gave us a highly distorted model of primate society as it exists in the wild. It was not until the work of various scientists in the animals' natural settings that we had any real insight into the workings of primate society. Psychologists have aptly shown that the nature of the testing procedure, in humans, often predicates the test results.

Social science in general, and anthropology in particular, derives its data from uncontrolled situations. The nature of the science is such that the situation cannot be replicated, nor can the theories derived therefrom be experimentally proven. There are so many variables that the theories themselves must be broadly stated. In fact, the enormous complexity of even the simplest cultures, coupled with the almost infinite variety of cultural expressions, led even the early anthropologists to despair of developing general "laws" or regularities of culture. Lowie's definition of culture as a thing of rags and patches and Boas's assertion that if there were any regularities in human society these must be sought on a psychological level are both examples of this early despair. However, these statements were made at a time when data was being collected at a pace which precluded organization, classification, and intensive study.

More recently, some anthropologists are attempting to build theories that can be applied to the study of cultures. Such, for example, is White's "law of general evolution." This states that through time, culture as a whole has tended to go from the simple to the complex, from small to larger. Certainly this proposition neatly fits Agassiz's third statement; it is self-evident. Never, in earlier times, did man exist in such great numbers as he does today. Never before have societies been so complex. Yet even here we can find exceptions. There are still Bushmen living in the Kalahari Desert as small hunting bands. Tribal societies live in Africa and the American Southwest. Examples such as these would once have been gleefully cited as negative instances, only one of which was deemed necessary to disprove a theory. They reflect, however, not the fallibility of the theory, but rather a lack of understanding of the nature of scientific theory on the part of the critic.

Today, we recognize that the greater the number of uncontrolled variables in a situation, the less accurate any prediction as to the outcome can be. Therefore, any science that examines data under less than the absolute control of the laboratory situation must express its findings in terms of mathematical percentages of probability. You find this now in weather reporting, where the day's forecast is no longer stated as "rain today, clearing tomorrow," but as "60 percent chance of rain today, 20 percent chance of rain tomorrow."

This thesis has been stated for physics in Heisenberg's "principle of indeterminacy." Specifically, the principle states the inability to predict the order in which atoms in a radioactive substance will decay. A simple example of this is the following: when we set a kettle of water on the stove, we know that when a certain temperature is reached, the water will boil, but we do not know which molecule of water will be the first to turn into steam.

Applied to White's theory of general evolution, this implies that although culture as a *whole* tends to go from the simple to

6

the complex, and from the small to the large, it would be very difficult to predict accurately how individual cultures will change. This is not very satisfying to those of us who are interested in a particular culture at a given time. However, anthropologists are working to define the variables that modify development of individual cultures. When these variables can be understood, anthropology's ability to predict change in individual cultures will improve.

In sum, anthropology is a social science in the process of building theories regarding the nature of man's cultures. It proceeds through the stages of hypothesis, data collection and analysis, and proposal of a theory. As a new science, these theories are few and broadly stated. Through time, these theories will be tested against reality, refined, augmented, or changed. As our knowledge grows, we will be able, within limits, to predict the course of culture change.

# CHAPTER 2

# Would That God
# the Giftie Gie Us

When poet Robert Burns wrote the line that is used as the chapter title, he was talking about one of the phenomena of being human—the inability to see ourselves or our culture objectively. Western man has a tendency to regard himself as a species apart from nature. He tends to regard his own society's way of life as "normal" and "right." We can never hope to understand and solve our problems until we recognize our place among the species. Nor can we hope to live peaceably among our neighbors until we accept the idea that there are quite reasonable alternatives to our way of doing things. This kind of objectivity is the goal of anthropology.

## What Is an Anthropologist?

Among the social sciences, anthropology is that science which is concerned with the study of man from his origins to the present and with his cultures as expressed all over the world. The anthropologist is concerned with man as a biological entity. He studies the origin of man, his fossil history, and the genetic components of the various populations that make up present-day humanity. In his search to understand our common primate heritage, he takes to the field to study primate societies. A specialist in this area is called a *physical anthropologist*.

Since not all societies survive into modern times, the anthropologist is interested in studying the remains of societies that no longer exist and that left no written records we can translate. We are concerned with the artifacts, the things left behind, insofar as they lead us to an understanding of the way of life of the people. The anthropologist who does this type of work is an *archaeologist*.

Anthropologists who study language, are, of course, anthropological *linguists*. They are concerned with the nature of the language used in a given culture. Linguists have added to our knowledge scores of languages spoken by small groups of people in nonwestern societies. They are also concerned with the derivations of languages and their changes through time.

By far, most anthropologists are *cultural anthropologists*. These are the scientists who study the cultures of men in all their variety.

## What Is Culture?

When the anthropologist uses the word *culture*, he refers to something quite different from the generally accepted use of the term. We often think of culture in terms of sophisticated tastes in music, art, or literature. But the anthropologist is concerned with something more sweeping. To the anthropologist, culture may be defined as all learned patterns of thought and behavior characteristic of a population or society. Culture, then, is learned behavior of all kinds. It includes, as Tylor's definition originally had it, arts and artifacts, beliefs and traditions. Culture is distinctive to each society. It is learned by humans as members of their societies.

Culture, in this sense, has a number of chracteristics universal to the phenomenon. For one thing, culture is *cumulative*. This is easy to see when we examine technology. The automobile, such an important part of our culture, is based on inventions and discoveries made long ago. The invention of the wheel, for example, was a necessary prelude to the development of the automobile. The discovery of the use of fire, too, was an important component. The wheel was invented during the Neolithic period, or New Stone Age, which started about 10,000 years ago, and the use of fire goes back possibly 800,000 years.

In a later chapter, when we discuss the technologies of various societies, we will see that invention and innovation were relatively slow during earlier periods. We also recognize that, in modern times, invention follows upon invention with bewildering rapidity. This is an expression of the fact that as culture accumulates, there is a greater backlog of knowledge and a greater possibility of reorganizing that knowledge in order to solve current problems. That is what invention really is: the reassessment, reorganization, and application of known facts to solve a particular problem.

For this reason, many instances of simultaneous discovery or invention must be expected. As a level of cultural accretion is reached, people in many parts of the world who have similar problems will solve those problems in similar ways. We have only to recognize the simultaneous discovery of natural selection by both Wallace and Darwin, the nearly simultaneous discovery of the use of insulin in England and the United States, and a host of similar simultaneous inventions. Invention and innovation are not really so much the expression of a particular human being's genius, although that may be the case, as they are an expression of the cultural accumulation of a particular time.

In addition to being cumulative, culture can also be said to be *transgenerational.* Culture can be passed not only from parents to children, as is the case with inherited characteristics, but also from child to parent, and even between people who share neither the same space nor the same time. By turning to your library, you can read the works of people who are long dead, or who, though alive in your time, live a great distance from you. Culture can be transmitted much more rapidly than biological traits, and also more variably.

The transmission of culture is through learning; however, this type of learning takes place so subtly that anthropologists use other terms to describe the process. An individual absorbs the ways of his native specific society gradually, informally as well as formally, and so completely that he comes to regard these ways as "natural." This process is called *enculturation.*

Enculturation includes not only the obvious patterns, such as language, food preferences, the uses of artifacts, and so forth. It also includes role behavior and reaction expectations. If, in our society, a father is supposed to support his children, we regard such support as expected behavior from the person we address as "father." And, indeed, that person usually conforms to that expectation. However, there are societies in which support is a function of the person addressed as "mother's brother," and "father" is someone who plays with and teases the children but neither supports nor disciplines them. To the anthropologist, fatherly behavior is not a matter of biology, but a matter of culture.

What seems "natural" to the encultured person is learned behavior. Even the role of mothering, which in our society has often been regarded as so natural as to be called "instinct," differs from society to society. In some cultures, the mother's sisters or the father's other wives perform the mothering function. In Western society, often an unrelated person such as a nurse or a "nanny" is more intimately concerned with the baby's welfare than is the biological mother.

The fact that culture is learned behavior, transgenerationally transmitted, is neatly shown by the phenomenon of *acculturation*. This term is used by the anthropologist to mean the learning of a new culture by people who have already been encultured in another culture. Most of our forebears, at some time, became accultured to the American culture. All of us have at one time or another witnessed the struggles of an immigrant to cope with the perplexities of the new way of life. The degree to which the individual succeeds in coping is a factor of both his individual abilities and the help he is given.

In some countries, where attempts are being made to acculture indigenous folk populations to modern society, the transgenerational aspect of culture is evident in the number of children who attempt to teach reading and writing to illiterate parents, and in the conscious attempt to change dietary and child-rearing methods through indoctrination of schoolchildren, who are expected to transmit this learning to their elders.

The fact that culture is learned behavior and not biologically based is shown by the fact that people of all races, ages, and sexes have successfully become accultured to societies other than their native ones. A striking example of this was shown by Darwin himself. During the voyage of the H.M.S. *Beagle,* Darwin had the opportunity to meet a society of people called the Yahgan. These people live at the tip of South America, in Tierra del Fuego. They are notable for the sparcity of their cultural inventory. They keep themselves warm by constantly burning fires in lieu of clothing or adequate shelter. Their means of subsistence depends on fishing and hunting sea mammals from rather leaky boats. Darwin took a little girl from this society and brought her back to Queen Victoria's court where she was promptly named Posy and provided with tutors, governesses, and all the paraphernalia necessary to a proper British upbringing. As a result, this child became a model of English propriety and a popular and successful member of the British court.

The example of Posy points to what is perhaps the most significant trait of the concept of culture. This is defined best by Ashley Montagu (1968), who calls culture man's *adaptive dimension.* First, a word of caution about the word *adaptation.* Too often, we fail to distinguish between long-term adaptation and short-term adaptation. Short-term adaptation is inevitably expedient. It is a way of coping with given conditions. Once those conditions change, as all things do through time, the formerly adaptive strategy may become neutral in survival value, or may become maladaptive.

With this in mind, we can examine Montagu's observation more closely. Let us take a situation that occurred regularly during man's early history on earth. Man evolved during the Pleistocene period, when the earth was subjected to periodic lowering of temperatures, which we call the Ice Ages. Other animals, faced with lowered world temperatures, attempted to cope by migrating to warmer climates. Often, this involved great hardship and heavy casualties, and sometimes the animals became extinct before the trek was completed. The only way an animal could adapt to a change of climate was through the lucky happenstance of a mutation in the breeding population, producing an animal that was better adapted to the new climate either through a metabolic change or a heavier pelt. By the time such a mutation became pervasive enough to be significant in the survival of the species, the species might well have become extinct, or the climatic conditions might have changed. This is particularly the case with animals that have long periods of pregnancy, or gestation, and sexual immaturity, coupled with infrequent breeding seasons. Although man has no breeding season, as such—and this may well have been an adaptation to this kind of situation—he does have a long gestation period and a long period of infancy and childhood before he is sexually mature. How then did he survive? As everyone who has ever seen a picture of "cavemen" can tell you, he slung an animal pelt over himself and retreated to his cave, either before or after learning the art of keeping fire. Clothing, shelter, and the use of fire are all items of culture. They do not depend on accidents of biology. They can be learned and, once learned, can be transmitted formally or informally in a short space of time. Man does not have any formidable bodily defenses or weapons; he has neither claw nor fang, nor is he a particularly swift or agile runner. How did he defend himself against predators? He presumably used stone tools to fashion weapons of wood or stone. Tools and weapons are items of the cultural inventory.

Since culture is learned behavior, it follows that what is adaptive and learned can, if it proves maladaptive in the long term, be unlearned. Although this appears simple logic, it has yet to be demonstrated that mankind behaves according to logic. Many people, particularly the young, witnessing the variety of problems we badly fumble because of "traditional" attitudes, have reason to doubt the validity of culture as an adaptive mechanism. We are faced here with the problem of long-term versus short-term adaptability and with the factor of cultural persistence inherent in the concept of culture as cumulative. Many traits and attitudes we retain were adaptive at one time, but with changing conditions they are so no longer. And yet, because of the cumulative nature of culture, these traits and attitudes persist.

There is no rule in the game of nature that states that our culture, or for that matter, the human species, must win out in the end. If we do not succeed in reconciling cultural continuity with adaptiveness, we will fail. In such reconciliation lies our best hope. Such a balance can only be reached through intensive study of culture as a whole and of the systems that comprise individual cultures. This is the job of the anthropologist.

It is not only the cultural anthropologist who is concerned in this process; each of the four branches of anthropology contributes its particular expertise to the study of the whole. Anthropologists, therefore, speak of their discipline as *holistic,* in that it treats of all aspects of mankind. Anthropologists also tend to do their work in interdisciplinary settings. Archaeologists, for example, include the findings of geologists, botanists, paleontologists, soil chemists, biologists, and physicists in their reports. Often, these specialists are called into the field; at other times, they do their job in the laboratory on samples supplied by the archaeologist. A study of a given culture by a cultural anthropologist may include provision for working with historians, sociologists, psychologists, and linguists, among others. There is no area exclusively marked "for anthropologists only." Indeed, the work of the sociologist in a complex urban society often overlaps with the anthropologist doing "urban anthropology." The unique quality the anthropologist brings to his chosen work is his methodology.

### Anthropological Method

Anthropological method is based upon model-building. The model-building process must start with an intimate and insightful knowledge of a particular society. Toward this end, one of the traditional aspects of the training of an anthropologist consists of *field work.* This means leaving office and library and going off to live for a period of time in a culture you want to study. The culture is selected, ideally, because it presents the type of problem the anthropologist is interested in studying. More realistically, it may be chosen for such reasons as accessibility, the fact that the particular culture may be on the verge of extinction, or that the anthropologist is asked to join a team already going to a particular place for another purpose.

Whatever the reason, once the anthropologist is in the field, he does his work as a *participant-observer*. He lives among the people. He attempts to learn their language. He eats their food and, where possible, shares in their joys and sorrows. He gets to know them. Usually he (or she) will find some member of the culture who has the patience, friendliness, and interest to take the anthropologist under his wing and introduce him to the intricacies of the culture. Such a person is called an *informant*. A delightful compilation of character studies of their favorite informants by a variety of anthropologists is available in Casagrande's book, *In the Company of Man* (1960).

Living in this way, the anthropologist gets to know the culture from the inside, as it were. The term for this inside view of a culture is *emic*. One cannot really grasp the fine details of a culture unless one is able to live in it. Certainly, for the scientist, living in a culture is as necessary as experimenting in a lab. The emic view, then, is the way people, including the participant anthropologist, see their own culture. The observer, still the anthropologist, brings in the *etic* view. Etic observation means the way the culture appears to an outsider. The anthropologist is both a participant and an observer because in his person he combines the emic and the etic views. He derives the emic view by living in the culture. He derives the etic view because, despite his term of residence, he is still an encultured member of his own society, and he brings to his studies a degree of objectivity not often achieved by a member of that culture.

The importance of both these viewpoints toward obtaining a fuller understanding of a society is shown neatly by the work of Roy Rappaport in New Guinea. In his book, *Pigs for the Ancestors,* Rappaport (1968) examines a particular feast that occurs among the Tsembaga people. A great many pigs are slaughtered; a good deal of ritual accompanies the distribution of food, and the general tenor of the occasion is of a great ceremony to honor the dead and venerated ancestors. If you ask a Tsembaga why he participates in this feast, you are told that he is honoring his ancestors and storing up their goodwill which is so necessary to the continued good health and prosperity of the society. This is the emic view. Rappaport himself observed that these feasts are usually held at the time of year when the new crops are just beginning to sprout, a time when the semi-wild pigs which rove the village are most destructive. By uprooting the new green shoots, they threaten the harvest. When the pigs become most numerous and bothersome, the cry goes up for a "feast for the ancestors." This, then, can be seen etically, as a way of minimizing the damage to the potential crop at its most vulnerable time by a community ritual that destroys many of the pigs. Both the emic and the etic view are necessary to an understanding of the ritual. Few people have the necessary detachment to view activities in their own societies in this way. That is why the anthropologist provides a particular and necessary viewpoint.

The second step in anthropological method is *comparison*. Here, the anthropologist, back from the field, compares his notes, films, and tapes with the work of other anthropologists who have either worked in the same area or have examined the same problem in another area. As anthropology itself becomes older, the basis for comparison grows. There are now instances of anthropologists who have revisited the same society at frequent intervals and can document adaptive changes, development, or decay in the particular society they studied. Margaret Mead (1956), in her studies of the Manus, has documented the change over one lifetime from a stone-age society to an independent, emerging nation.

In other instances, two anthropologists who have visited the same people at different times can work together toward a study of the people that has greater time-depth than the usual study. Such is the case with Hart and Pilling (1960), who studied the Tiwi of Australia. Furthermore, the comparison of field data is now facilitated by the sophisticated use of film and tape recordings made in the field. These modern techniques have made the collection of ethnographic data far more reliable than ever before. Such compilations as the Human Relations Area Files, a microfilmed index of data collected by anthropologists all over the world, because they are cross-indexed, enable the anthropologist to compare one society by area or by trait with many others.

The final step in the anthropological method is the final step for most scientific processes: the drawing of a conclusion, a hypothesis. Again, in the light of what has been said, these hypotheses are tentative and subject to revision with better data and techniques. Nonetheless, they are an important step in the building of scientific theory. The search for regular processes in the development of cultures is as important to the survival of mankind as the search for disease-producing organisms.

## Ethnocentrism and Cultural Relativism

However, the search for such regularities is too often impeded by the mental set of non-anthropological investigators. Too often, non-anthropological accounts of exotic peoples are fraught with *ethnocentrism*. As explained earlier, people become so gradually and thoroughly encultured into the ways of their own society that they tend to think of those ways as right and the ways of other people as wrong, or natural as opposed to unnatural behavior. Each group, for example, thinks of itself as a chosen people. The translation of the word *Eskimo* is "human," inferring that non-Eskimos are not human. The same is true of the name *Navajo*, "the people," as opposed to others who are not people. Even the starving California Indian found cowering in a stockyard, his people dead, his band destroyed—even he, when asked his name, said, "Ishi," which means "the man" (T. Kroeber 1961). In our highly developed society, it is very easy to feel this kind of pride, because we see ourselves as infinitely more "successful" than most other people. Consequently, we take upon ourselves the burden of correcting almost everyone else's nutrition, politics, religion.

This view stems, in part, from the belief that there is only one right way, as opposed to several wrong ways, and this, in turn, stems from the misunderstanding of the evolutionary process in terms of survival of the fittest. We know now that Darwin's concept of "fittest" does not apply to daily life. There are no *fittest;* there are only the fit and the unfit. There are many varieties and degrees of fitness and unfitness. In fact, it would be fair to say "relatively fit" as compared to "relatively unfit." And the question must be asked, fit for what? Darwin was talking about species of animals, and his fitness was measured in terms of reproduction.

It was the sociologist Spencer who applied the Darwinian concept to culture and used it to justify the many inhumanities practiced at the start of the industrial revolution. We may, as we shall see, evaluate cultures on the basis of technological efficiency, or quality of life, or compatibility with our life-styles, or even artistic virtuosity. According to the standard chosen and the individual doing the choosing, each culture may be ranked quite differently on different points. In his training, the anthropologist has learned that every culture is an adaptive system, and each culture that survives, whether you approve of it or not, is adapted, and therefore a success. This attitude is embodied in the term *cultural relativism*.

The basic functions of a cultural system are to feed and reproduce its members with a degree of order. One needs order to structure the relationships that make food acquisition and reproduction possible. Any culture that manages to do this in its own particular environment, given its own peculiar history, is a relatively fit culture. Turnbull (1966) reports that in Africa, the Pygmies of the Ituri forest are a fit culture, whereas the Ik of the mountains are not fit, and Turnbull fears that the Ik will disappear as a cultural entity, though individuals may survive as part of other cultures.

Our way is not the only way and, in fact, may not be the best way. Certainly it is not the best way for people living under entirely different circumstances.

In an interview published in the *New York Times* of May 1973, the wife of President Marcos of the Philippines put it well when she explained why her husband declared martial law. Although her motives may be suspect, her explanation struck a responsive chord. She said the Philippines had tried the American version of democracy, and it didn't work. The country was crime-ridden, the officials corrupt, the people unhappy. "It is as though you gave me your coat," she said. "In my climate it would be too hot to wear, and besides it would be too long. I would have to alter it a great deal to be able to use it." Before we export our political or religious philosophies, we must remember that a culture is a system, and any change in one of the aspects of the system reverberates throughout.

We have not yet taken the measure of the relative fitness of our culture. What may appear to be remarkable short-term efficiency may, in the end, turn out to be long-term inefficiency. We cannot measure our worth, in an existence of only a few hundred years, against societies which have existed for thousands of years. It is sheer arrogance to instigate change, whether technological, political, or religious, into ongoing societies.

Before any attempts are made to change a culture, not only do we have to understand the cultural process, but we must understand that particular culture. The only real way to know a culture is to live in it, and at the same time to maintain a degree of objectivity. Even anthropologists, trained to be objective, find this difficult. Most of us are beset at sometime in our field experience by the phenomenon of *culture shock*.

On entering a strange culture, one is sharply aware of unfamiliar sounds, smells, tastes, and behaviors. Things seem to be unlike any we have earlier experienced. One can find few patterned regularities, and many things might initially seem remarkably unpleasant. Often, the anthropologist is so over-whelmed by these differences that he despairs of surviving, let alone accomplishing his work. Evans-Pritchard (1940) felt this way among the Nuer people, and Turnbull (1972) among the Ik. There is nothing one can grasp as familiar, and it is frightening. Customs and habits are different. The shock of an American mother watching a French child drink wine can only be matched by that of a Chinese mother watching an American drink milk. To the Chinese, milk is an excretion of the cow and is not potable. All this adds up to a feeling of such instability that it is best described by the term "shock."

The second stage in culture shock is a gradual realization that some of these strange customs are quite comfortable. This applies most readily to the siesta in hot climates, or nude bathing, or sleeping in a hammock instead of a bed. One begins to see some sense in the local customs and begins to use them. It is at this point that the stranger starts to make a judgment. Often, he finds the life of the people he is visiting so comfortable that they become "his" people, like the squaw-man of the American frontier who found comfort in the Indian way of life and consciously chose to follow it. Others, returning to their own cultures, retain a special fondness for the place and people they visited and find the return home something of a readjustment.

One of the causes of many misjudgments Western society has made in relation to other parts of the world is the fact that so few members of our society have lived in other parts of the world. Even where industry, the army, and the State Department have set up enclaves within foreign countries, these enclaves often remain isolated from the host country. The people within the enclave continue to speak their native tongue, eat their traditional food, attend their separate schools, and socialize among themselves. They have minimal contact with the "natives." It is often possible that a student of anthropology who has never set foot in a particular culture will understand it better than a diplomat who may have "lived" there for ten years or more. Yet policy-making is not in the hands of the anthropologist but rests with the diplomat.

One of the most important concepts anthropology has to offer is that of cultural relativism. We must, if we are to survive as a people, train ourselves to conquer our ethnocentricity and recognize that every culture surviving in the world today has validity. Each is fully as worthy of respect as our own. It has adapted to its own history and its own environment. Any attempt to tinker with it and impose our own political, religious, or

economic structures upon another society is potentially destructive of that other cultural system. Our ethnocentricity is self-
defeating, as well, in that it prevents us from recognizing
potentially valuable alternatives to our own life-style and potential solutions to some of our problems.

# CHAPTER 3

# The Naked Ape

In light of the previous discussion about the meaning of the word *theory*, we will now proceed to explore the process and theory of evolution as applied to man. Harris (1971 p. 633) defines evolution as "the change from an earlier form or entity into a later form or entity by means of cumulative modification."

In 1758, Linnaeus classified species of animals, starting with the simplest form and continuing through more complex forms to the primates, among which he included man. Linnaeus had no concept of process, nor did he suggest any connection among the species. In his time, species were believed to be unchanging, and the Biblical version of the origin of man was refined by Bishop Usher, who stated that man was created in the year 4004 B.C. In fact, Buffon, writing shortly after the Linnean classification system was published, said that one could infer a relationship between apes and men and, for that matter, between horses and donkeys, but since the Bible said this was not so, it must not be inferred.

All through the late 1700s and the early 1800s, geologists, biologists, and such wonderful "amateurs" as Boucher de Perthes continued to bring forth evidence of earlier strata of rocks and the existence of fossils so placed in these strata that they had to be accepted as having antiquity. The existence of such forms as fossil horses and fossils of animals no longer alive were explained by the orthodox as antedeluvial forms—species that existed before the flood of Noah. This theory was known as *catastrophism*.

Charles Lyell, the English geologist, in 1835 proposed the theory of *uniformitarianism*. This stated that there was an orderly progression from the simpler species to the more complex ones, and that the differences between fossil forms and modern ones could not be due to floods, fires, or other natural upheavals. Lyell saw the relationship between fossil forms and living forms, but he could not supply the mechanism by which this occurred.

It was not until the publication of Darwin's *On the Origin of Species* in 1859 that we have the postulation of a force which could account for the process of evolution, namely, *natural selection*. Between 1859 and 1871, when Darwin published *The Descent of Man*, the world was torn by conflict between those who upheld the church's view of special creation and those who accepted the Darwinian view. This led to some painful conflicts within scientists themselves, who were products of orthodox religious training. Some accepted the idea of the origin of species for other animals but rejected the view for man. A modern case in point is Pierre Teilhard de Chardin, who refers to "the Rubicon" crossed by man and regards man's particular gifts as indicative of special creation of his soul, if not his body, though he willingly accepts evolution for other forms of life. Rudolf Virchow, the noted German scientist, when shown a Neanderthal skull, diagnosed it as a pathological specimen of modern man. Nevertheless, the Darwinian hypothesis spurred an interest in fossil men, and since 1890, with the identification of the Pithecanthropus form in Java and, later, recognition of Neanderthal and Australopithecine forms, the fossil evidence for man's evolution has been collecting at a swift rate.

### Natural Selection

Let us examine now the process by which evolution took place, and continues to take place.

We must first state that an individual, as such, does not evolve. Individuals change and vary, but only populations evolve. Evolution, then, is first of all a process dependent on the existence of a *breeding population*. A breeding population is one in which there is free and random intermating. Any such population, be it men, mice, birds, or any other sexually reproducing organism, contains variety within the population. If it did not, one would be unable to distinguish individuals in the population.

These variations are caused by several factors. For one thing, every individual is a random sample of the genes of his parents and forebears. Since these ancestors are random samples of their ancestors, it would be more correct to state that the individual is a random sample of the entire pool of genes available to that breeding population. The recombination of those genes makes for variability within a population.

Variation also occurs due to the breakage and linkage of chromosomes during the process of egg and sperm formation. There are many individual differences due to the way the expression of a gene may be altered by environmental factors, such as illness or famine, but these do not concern us at this point. Differences in population are only significant to evolution if they are *heritable*—if one person can genetically transmit a trait to his children.

This variability is increased by the factor known as *mutation*. In every breeding population, some changes in the genetic material will occur randomly. This occurs at a regular rate in nature. Thus, even a relatively homogeneous population will, through time, show a degree of variability. These variations are random, not singled out for any logical reason. They are not oriented toward any goal, and they occur without any direction. They are the result of chance. Where they are major in nature, involving major changes in the form of the individual, they may indeed be lethal. When, however, these changes are minor, they do not interfere with the individual's ability to survive and reproduce. They therefore remain in the pool of genes that may be transmitted to the next generation.

A breeding population, which contains variety, is constantly being exposed to selection. It was the discernment of the process of natural selection which enabled Darwin to theorize the process by which species evolve. There has been considerable refinement of this concept since its inception. For one thing, we now recognize that the process of natural selection is not so drastic as to weed out all but the fittest. For another, we recognize that, in the case of man, differing rates of reproduction, which is all natural selection implies, may be culturally induced. We tend to think of the evolution of man, therefore, as being due to both cultural selection and natural selection. The concept of natural selection, however, still stands as the way evolution of species occurs.

*Natural selection* states that among the variations in a breeding population there may be some hereditary characteristics that confer upon the individual the ability to reproduce more frequently than can other individuals who do not possess these characteristics. This can be done simply by conferring upon an individual the greater possibility of surviving to maturity, of perhaps being more fertile, being fertile for a longer period of time, or of having greater success in attracting mates. It must be understood that these advantages only hold in given circumstances. If you like, selection is *conservative,* because it favors adaptation to a particular set of conditions. We speak of selection as being opportunistic, because natural selection selects for a better adaptation to a particular environment at a particular time. Again, there is no master plan here. Long-range trends can only be seen after many mutations have led to a change in form. And long-range trends are only possible if the environment remains stable. Any shift in the environment will engender a shift in the selective criteria.

Finally, a successful adaptation, by breeding in greater numbers, expands its territorial range and may filter into new areas, where different environmental criteria apply. It will then be selected according to different criteria, and after a time this new group will vary significantly from its parent population. This is the process we call *adaptive radiation.* It should be noted that because selection is far less drastic than implied in the notion of "survival of the fittest," the population will always contain sufficient variety so that further changes can occur. When a trend in a given population has continued over so long a time that a notably different variety emerges, we can speak of an evolutionary change. In the same way, when a variety radiates into a new environment and becomes measurably different from the parent population, we can also speak of an evolutionary change, as we will see in the evolution of the pepper moth.

Depending upon the lifespan of the organism and the breeding rate of the species, evolution can be a relatively short or long process. Man has a very long lifespan compared to fruit flies. And man's reproductive cycle is relatively slow compared to rabbits. So it is not surprising that evolutionary changes in man should require relatively long periods of time. Furthermore, trends in evolution are not always readily apparent. The past 40,000 years, for example, have marked a period of progressive decalcification, or thinning of the bones, in man, as well as a marked reduction in tooth and jaw size. There are probably also marked changes in body chemistry, metabolic rates, and so forth, which, although they do not appear obvious, do mark definite evolutionary trends.

### Continuing Evolution

Since these evolutionary changes are relatively small, there are people who declare that evolution has ceased, as far as man is concerned, nor can they see evidence for continuing evolution even in animal populations. These persons are wrong on all counts. In a later chapter, we will be discussing the trends in the continuing evolution of man and new adaptive stresses that are making their appearance. In terms of other species, the newer forms of pests, such as microbes resistant to antibiotics, are sufficient evidence of continuing evolution. More dramatic, perhaps, at least visually, is the evolution of the pepper moth of England.

The pepper moth comes in two varieties, a light moth and a dark moth. Until recently, the light moths far outnumbered the dark ones. This was probably because birds fed on these moths, and the light moth perched against a light tree-trunk was less visible than the dark moth. With the increased industrialization of England, tree trunks have become darkened with soot, so now the dark moth has protective coloration, and its percentage in the population is now larger than the light moth's. If this trend persists, pepper moths may eventually all be dark, and a new form will have emerged through cumulative modification. That is how evolution works.

Man, then, presents variety in his population. These varieties are acted upon by natural selection and specifically, in man, by cultural selection.

## Cultural Selection

*Cultural selection* implies that man's culture sets up conditions that produce different rates of reproduction based upon cultural criteria. The distinction between natural and cultural selection is difficult to make, because both processes are simultaneously at work. However, when early man had less control over his environment, certain physical characteristics, such as keen vision, muscular strength, agility, and endurance were important to his survival and no doubt were influential in mate selection and reproduction. In some societies, such as the Masai of Africa, until recently a man could not marry unless he had proven his ability to kill a lion.

In modern industrial society, survival and mate selection are based upon quite different criteria. Poor vision can be ameliorated through the use of eyeglasses, and education, status, and temperament now play a greater role than physical strength in ensuring both survival and mate selection. Man is in the unique position of having domesticated himself, so to speak, because he set up, through the operation of culture, his own criteria of selection.

As we examine the forms of fossil man, we are impressed by two physical trends made possible by culture. The first is progressive thinning of the bones. As man was able to create a safer environment and use tools, dexterity and agility had more survival value than sheer brute strength. As man became able to cook his food, heavy jaws and teeth no longer had the survival value that they had earlier. The second noticeable trend is the rapid growth of the brain. This probably is the result of a feedback among language, tool making, and ingenuity—the mental capacity for innovation. Among other animals, nature selects for physical and mental characteristics. Man, uniquely, selects for criteria useful to himself. He does this when he domesticates other animals. Evidently, however unconsciously, he has done this with his own development, thus being the only animal capable of setting up the criteria of selection.

Finally, through both technology and population growth, man has spread all over the earth, and even into the ocean's depths and into outer space, if only for short periods of time. This spread has engendered further changes in the selective criteria and in the degree of variety present, in that, as we shall discuss later, new races are being created, even as old ones are being absorbed. Man is indeed evolving through adaptive radiation.

### History of Fossil Man

Remembering, then, that man is a relatively slow-breeding animal, and that evolution proceeds by cumulative modification rather than by major leaps, we should expect to pick up the beginnings of man's evolution at a remote time in the past. And so we do. The story goes back some twenty million years. The earlier part of the story, the evolution of the *prosimians*, those early primates which preceded the monkeys, occurred earlier still and will not be covered in this book, although the fascinating story is readily available in any good biology text.

As long ago as 1856, fragments of jaws and teeth from a very ancient group of *primates*, that class of animals containing monkeys, apes, and man, were being collected from Europe, Africa, India, and China, in both fossil and modern form. A *fossil* is the remains of an ancient form. Each fossil was given a unique name, and each was often assigned to a different genus (Buettner-Janusch 1966:122–127). It was not until the work of Pilbeam and Simons in 1965 that these fossils were studied as a unit and a coherent classification emerged. These primates are now designated as *Dryopithecines,* primates which lived some twenty million years ago and which are regarded as ancestral to both apes and men.

As would be expected in a form undergoing rapid adaptive radiation, many varieties of Dryopithecines existed. These have been classified into three groups: Dryopithecus, Ramapithecus and Gigantopithecus. Ramapithecus (see Figure 1) has been assigned to the family Hominidae, which includes man. Dryopithecus and Gigantopithecus have been assigned to the family Pongidae, making them ancestral to the apes. These classifications have been assigned primarily on the basis of *dentition,* which means the number and kinds of teeth the animal has. No reputable scientist presumes that man is descended from the apes, even though much of our behavior seems similar to theirs. There is no "missing link." Apes and men had a common ancestor, the Dryopithecines.

We come now to the more recent periods, and the evolution of the hominids, leading to and including modern man. The geologic period during which this development took place is the Pleistocene, a period marked by wide variations of climate that

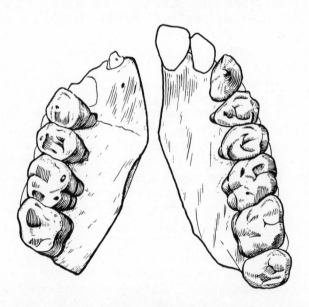

FIGURE 1. *Ramapithecus:* palate and teeth, after Simons, as represented by the original fragment from India (left) and Kenyapithecus from Africa, combined. (From *Mankind in the Making,* copyright 1959, 1967 by William Howells. Reprinted by permission of Doubleday & Company, Inc.)

we call the Ice Ages. In Europe, several glacial periods are distinguished. These glacial periods were separated by long periods of relatively mild climate. These interglacial periods are measured in terms of a hundred thousand years, in some cases, while the glacial periods themselves cover tens of thousands of years. As implied in the term, "Ice Age," the temperature was considerably lower during periods of glaciation, but perhaps equally significant for the development of man was the fact that during the glacial periods, water, which would normally have covered land areas, was frozen into glaciers, thus lowering the sea levels. For long periods of time man had relatively unimpeded access to places that at other times were under water. This is important to bear in mind when we discuss the location of the various fossil finds and the differentiation among breeding populations.

## Australopithecus

Since the first discovery, in 1924, by R. A. Dart of the hominid called *Australopithecus* (see Figure 2), many finds of this type have been made by investigators. Unfortunately, each find has been distinctively named instead of classified with other finds, and only recently, through the work of Brace and others (1971), have attempts been made to straighten out the terminology. Thus, we have Zinjanthropus, Paranthropus, Telananthropus, and other fossils. They are all here subsumed, following Brace, into the category of the Australopithecines. Most of the finds are from Africa, ranging through the whole eastern part of the continent, north and south, and there is some possibility of their existence also in Java and China.

We used to think of Australopithecus as existing in two varieties: a heavy-boned, robust type, and a smaller, slimmer variety. More recent evaluation has led Brace and his colleagues (1971:20) to propose that the robust type is male and the slimmer and smaller type female, thus allowing for greater sexual dimorphism.

*Sexual dimorphism* refers to differences in physical appearance between sexes. In birds, for example, males and females of the same species may have differently colored plumage. In animals, males are usually larger, more muscular, and have a heavier coat of hair. These traits are important where the male protects the female and their young against predators. The Australopithecines, having no great development of tools and

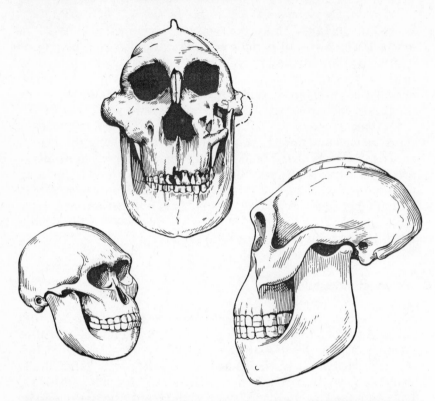

FIGURE 2. Skulls of the Australopithecinae. Center, "Zinjanthropus" from Olduvai, a *Paranthropus,* from a photograph, with jaw supplied by modification of the Peninj specimen. Left, *Australopithecus* from Makapan, after the restoration by Dart. Right, *Paranthropus* from Swartkrans, based on various photographs and casts. Notable features of *Paranthropus* are the great jaw height and the short crest along the mid-line of the skull. (From *Mankind in the Making,* copyright 1959, 1967 by William Howells. Reprinted by permission of Doubleday & Company, Inc.)

weapons, must have relied heavily on the physical strength of the male for survival. The Australopithecines were about four to five feet tall, weighing fifty to one hundred pounds. They stood erect, and their pelvic structure differs very little from that of modern man. On the other hand, their brain capacity was no larger than that found in modern apes. The teeth are quite like ours, showing no·evidence of enlarged canine teeth as other forms have.

The Australopithecines are sometimes referred to as man-apes, primarily because of their small brain size and generally ape-like facial features. They should preferably be called pre-men or proto-men. They did walk erect on two legs (bipedal posture), and this fact alone assumes tremendous importance when we consider its implications. A quadrapedal (four-legged) animal has the advantage of being able to support the weight of its internal organs all along the spinal column. A biped, however, due to laws of gravity, carries most of its weight on the pelvic bones. This, besides causing us many backaches, also selects for a shortened and widened pelvis.

The wider pelvic bones, present in Australopithecus as well as in modern man, occur at the expense of the width of the birth canal. As a consequence, human infants are born smaller, relative to their adult size, and less mature than the young of other animals. In fact, the brain of a human baby at birth is not enclosed in a sealed bony case. The infant's brain is encased in plates of bone which have not solidified, and these slide over each other during the birth process. Thus, many human infants at birth seem to have malshaped heads, and when holding a human infant, we are cautioned about the soft spot at the top of the skull, where the brain is not protected by bone. It takes a year or more before the hole atop the head disappears or is covered over. This would be an enormous disadvantage to the survival of the infant were it not cared for by adults. Hence, while erect posture causes a degree of maladaptation, it also provides a means for alleviating the worst effects, for a bipedal animal can carry not only its infant but also food and water to the baby. Moreover, the fact that the infant is helpless for such a long time, and then dependent for an even longer time, allows opportunity for learning the culture unmatched by any other animal.

In sum, erect posture leads to development of the family, since presumably someone has to go out and hunt and gather while someone else is homebound caring for the child. It also provides for development of culture through the process we call enculturation. Although these traits may not have been well developed in Australopithecus, he had the physical characteristics necessary for their development, and he thus should be considered well within the direct ancestry of modern man.

Australopithecines roamed the earth for millions of years, each breeding population showing some variation from other breeding populations. However, to our knowledge, no population was so completely cut off from others, nor were such marked differences developed as to cause different groups to evolve into different species. There seems to have been a tendency, as time went on, for the individuals to become somewhat larger and for brain capacity to become larger, particularly the forebrain. The result of this cumulative modification was to show up about 800,000 years before the present time, in a new form, classified as *Homo erectus*. As you can see from the genus *Homo*, this type is fully accepted as man, a direct ancestor of modern man.

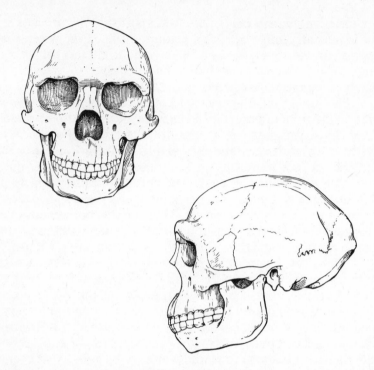

FIGURE 3. Pekin (or Peking) Man. Restoration of a female skull by Weiden-reich. After Weidenreich. (From *Mankind in the Making,* copyright 1959, 1967 by William Howells. Reprinted by permission of Doubleday & Company, Inc.)

## Homo Erectus

Before we explore the classification of the genus Homo (see Figure 3), it would be well to discuss the matter of classification in general, as it pertains to man.

One must classify if one is to order knowledge so as to understand nature. However, the order so imposed is bound to be arbitrary. When we are dealing with a rapidly evolving organism, particularly where the evolution is fairly recent, there are bound to be many intermediate forms whose classification will be a subject of controversy among specialists. Evolution, as we know, occurs as a result of cumulative modification. At what point in the continuum does one draw the line between *Homo erectus* and *Homo sapiens*?

Homo erectus ranged all over Europe and North Africa and is known from Java and China. One of the earliest discoveries of this fossil man was made in 1891 in Java by Dubois. Since that time, fossils have been found by several other anthropologists:

Leakey, Pei, Arambourg, and Henri-Martin. The variations in Homo erectus are so great that some fossils have created great arguments among classifiers. The classification used here is that suggested by Brace, Nelson, and Korn (1971).

The populations unquestionably classified as Homo erectus exhibit a variety in toolmaking traditions, as we shall see later. Certain changes are quite evident from the earlier Australopithecines. The average brain size was double that of the Australopithecines (Brace, et al. 1971). The molars of Homo erectus are smaller and are within the modern range of variation. At this stage of his development, man is still chinless. Fossils from Java give us only leg bones from Homo erectus. Based upon reconstruction from this single bone, Homo erectus, or perhaps just this individual, averaged between five feet, six inches and five feet, eight inches—much larger than the earlier Australopithecines. The development of a higher forehead is linked to the development of language and memory (Campbell 1972).

In 1973, a new chapter in the hunt for the lost remains of Peking Man opened. First discovered in Choukoutien, forty miles west of Peking, China, these fossils present the only known instance of fossil bones of Homo erectus which represent a whole community of people. Unfortunately, these bones, rightfully a national treasure of the Chinese people, were lost during World War II. Apparently they were packed in cases and sent to an American Marine base in China just as the Japanese overran the base. No one knows where they are now. The Chinese government has asked American cooperation in their recovery. Individuals who were at the American base when it was overrun claim that the case of bones may still be there. There is some evidence, however, that the case may have been loaded aboard an American ship at that time and taken out of China, perhaps to Russia according to recent reports. Or, the collection may have fallen into the hands of private individuals, because it has never turned up at any American museum or university. Harry Shapiro of the American Museum of Natural History has taken a personal interest in recovery of this treasure, not only because of its value to the Chinese, but also because, if found, it will add immeasurably to our knowledge of Homo erectus.

### Neanderthal Man

About 100,000 years ago, man had reached a point in cumulative modification which can be classed as another stage, that of *Homo*

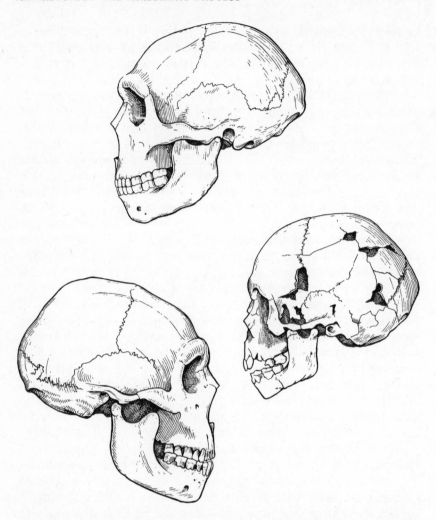

FIGURE 4. Neanderthal skulls. In the center is a restoration of the type of the "classic" Neanderthals, based on Monte Circeo, the best preserved, with jaw and teeth added from other specimens. Left, Shanidar skull as reconstructed by T. D. Stewart. Right, Teshik-Tash boy (right side reversed). (From *Mankind in the Making,* copyright 1959, 1967 by William Howells. Reprinted by permission of Doubleday & Company, Inc.)

*sapiens neandertalensis,* the familiar Neanderthal Man (see Figure 4). This form is known from sites all over the Old World, although no such forms are recognizable in this hemisphere. We know a great deal more about this form than we do about the earlier forms, because, being closer to us in time, there are more remains.

The brain size is as large or larger than that of modern man, and the name, *Homo sapiens neandertalensis,* tells us that this form is placed in the same class as modern man. However, the jaws and teeth are still as large (some even larger) as *Homo erectus.* Neanderthal still has no chin, and there is still relatively small development of modern man's high forehead. For these reasons, *Homo sapiens neandertalensis* is classified apart from modern man (*Homo sapiens sapiens*), although they belong to the same category.

The bony projections over the eyes and the general massive buttressing system of the skull shows the antiquity of a Neanderthal skull. Some physical anthropologists regard Neanderthal as a group of *Homo sapiens* specifically adapted to cold climate, rather than as a separate variety. Carleton Coon (1962:533) suggested that the short husky stature of Neanderthal is similar to that of modern Eskimo populations who live in frigid climates. The large nose, Coon suggests, may have acted to warm the cold air before it reached the lungs and the brain.

We are fortunate that two investigators, one working at Shanidar Cave in Iraq (Solecki 1971), and one working in Yugoslavia (Gorjanovic-Kramberger 1906), have both discovered populations of Neanderthals which give us a fair idea of the range of variety in the population. The range is from a type that has massive brow ridges, jaws, and teeth, which was formerly called "classic Neanderthal," to a far less extreme version which is so close to early *Homo sapiens sapiens* that "the distinction between Neanderthal and modern man is arbitrary, and since we take the position that modern form evolved from Neanderthal form, obviously there will be specimens dating from the time the change took place that will be difficult to put in either category" (Brace, et al. 1971:115).

This statement is all the more remarkable since the earliest finds of the Neanderthal form were of the "classic" variety and were not accepted as being directly ancestral to man. In fact, modern man's ethnocentricity led to a flight of the imagination in which Neanderthal, ugly, squat, and brutish, huddling in his vermin-ridden cave, was confronted by *Homo sapiens sapiens,* who, of course, was a handsome, athletic type. A great battle was fought, in which Neanderthal was exterminated and the world was freed for modern man. Needless to say, this fancy is not based upon a single shred of hard evidence. In fact, as the late Ernest Hooton, a physical anthropologist who taught at Harvard University, used to say, he found many Neanderthals present at his classes.

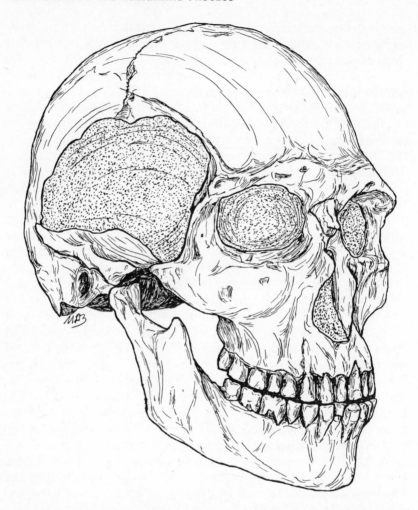

FIGURE 5. *Homo sapiens sapiens,* modern man. (From *Atlas of Fossil Man* by C. Loring Brace, Harry Nelson and Noel Korn. Copyright © 1971 by Holt, Rinehart and Winston, Inc. Reproduced by permission of Holt, Rinehart ond Winston, Inc.)

## Modern Man

Gradually, over a span of thousands of years, modern man emerged (see Figure 5). The prime difference between the more evolved Neanderthals and early *Homo sapiens sapiens* involve reduction of the bony buttressing system, reduction in tooth and jaw size, and the gradual development of a high forehead, because of the development of the frontal lobes of the brain. This

**34**

process still continues in our time. There is a progressive reduction of facial muscularity and robustness. Wiggling one's ears is now an oddity but everyone used to be able to do it.

We can set no date for the appearance of modern man; however, most anthropologists would agree to a time period of about 40,000 years ago as marking the period when such a form was already predominant. In the last 40,000 years, there has been continued evolution in the directions already stated. Our teeth and jaws have become progressively narrower. Our bones have become progressively thinner. Individuals now exist who have such thin skulls they would probably have perished in earlier times.

In conclusion, it should be stressed that man evolved slowly by cumulative modification from earlier forms. Man's ancestry can be traced back some twenty million years. We suffer not from too few fossils, but rather from the fact that there are so many fossil forms, and evolutionary change was so gradual, that absolute classification becomes difficult, even arbitrary. We should remember that, through time, in each of the stages, people had individual differences. It should be remembered that all of the varieties living at one time were capable of interbreeding and apparently did so. Man never evolved into more than one species, and he remains, in all his variety, a single species today.

# CHAPTER 4

# He Looks Just Like
# Uncle Joe

Having determined that man's body evolved from a primate form
which was also ancestral to present-day monkeys and apes, we
can ask whether there are any behavioral characteristics which
derive from some common ancestor. If that were so, it would be
presumed that such behavior might be present, however modified, among present-day apes and monkeys. Most of us recognize
some degree of kinship. Certainly people are fascinated by ex-
hibits of monkeys and apes in zoos. Their postures, antics, and
facial grimaces are amusing to us, perhaps because they are
familiar.

In the early 1960s, anthropologists recognized that studies
of primates carried on in zoos were akin to studying human
behavior in jails. They carried the participant-observer method a
step further and went into the field to do studies of monkeys
and apes in the wild. These field studies have resulted in data
that tend to refute many of the popular notions of our time.
Unfortunately, we have had a spate of books, some written by
specialists in animal behavior, others by amateurs, which tend to
generalize from animal behavior to human behavior. These books
have become popular because they tend to relieve present-day
man of responsibility for his actions by blaming our unpleasant
characteristics on our animal forebears. We shall discuss this
further in a later chapter.

Certainly, since anthropologists agree that man is classified
as an animal rather than a plant or a mineral, he would share
certain characteristics with other animals. However, millions of
years of evolution separate man from fish or from geese. It would

be highly unlikely to find behavior patterns in these animals that can be scientifically shown to be ancestral to man's behavior. Even the distance between monkeys and men is so great that one may properly ask whether there is anything in monkey behavior which is antecedent to man's social organization.

The answer appears to be that there is. In 1938, C. R. Carpenter (1964), a psychologist, imported rhesus monkeys from various locations in India and loosed them on a small island near Puerto Rico. Their behavior was totally chaotic. They fought and chased each other and generally rampaged to such an extent that Carpenter was unable to accomplish his research goals.

In 1956, another investigator, S. A. Altmann, revisited the island and found a peaceful natural habitat within which several colonies of rhesus monkeys were engaged in the business of living, in a fashion quite similar to their relatives at home in India (Southwick 1963:4). It seems that the monkeys, thrown together on the island, spent their first few years reestablishing a viable social organization, establishing a pecking order, and defining dominance positions. They were, it would seem, fighting and groping their way toward a new social organization, built around a new environment, and containing new individuals. The situation was not unlike that portrayed in the novel, *Lord of the Flies,* where young boys from a British school are shipwrecked on an island, and cruelly go through the pangs of establishing a pecking order (Golding 1959). It would seem, then, that monkeys, or at least rhesus monkeys, require some social organization in order to live in a peaceful fashion.

More recently, work in primate studies has been carried on with almost every type of ape and monkey. We shall confine ourselves to the studies of baboons and those of chimpanzees.


### Baboons

Technically, baboons are monkeys, not apes, and therefore further removed from us in the scale of evolution. But baboons have a particular trait that makes them of special interest to us—they spend most of their waking day on the ground, although they nest in trees for the night. Since we are also ground-living creatures, we might hope to find particular adaptations to this environment that are common to both baboons and man.

There are two species of baboons. One, the cynocephalus group, lives on the broad savannahs of Kenya and other parts of Africa. The other group, the hamadryas, live in the deserts of

Ethiopia. As would be expected, adaptation to differing environments has led to differing social systems, although there are broad similarities as well.

Scientists found that baboons in Kenya lived in groups ranging from ten to two hundred individuals (De Vore 1965). On the other hand, Ethiopian baboons lived in units in which one male herded several females, the units being part of a larger band which generally grazed and slept near each other (Kummer, in Jay 1968).

Although baboons do eat meat when they find it, they do not hunt and are primarily vegetarians. They spend their days grazing over a territory of three to six square miles. Unlike man, baboons are primarily quadrapedal (walking on four legs). They often resort to bipedal locomotion when the need arises, and they climb trees either to get at fruit or, nightly, to make sleeping nests. But most of their time is spent foraging for grass. This makes them vulnerable to the chief predator of their environment, the cheetah.

As a consequence, the baboons have developed a highly protective social organization. When the group is seen grazing, it can be noted that the savannah baboons are distributed in a definite order. In the center of the area are the dominant males. These are full adults who have established a pecking order among themselves but who act as a group in the defense of the troop (De Vore 1965 p.63). The dominant males are surrounded by females with young infants. Since females mature earlier than males, in a given troop at any one time, adult females outnumber the males. At the perimeter of the group are juvenile males who have not attained dominant status and older males who have been unable to maintain their dominance.

When a cheetah contacts a grazing group, the peripheral males are the first individuals threatened. They sound an alarm, and retreat, herding the females and infants with them. At the same time, the dominant males go forward to meet the threat. Sometimes a cheetah, met by a group of dominant males, has turned tail. The strength of the dominant group does not lie in the fighting ability of any one baboon but in their cohesiveness as a unit. Dominance is of a protective value to the entire troop. There is another facet of dominance behavior. The dominant males individually and collectively keep peace and order within the troop (De Vore 1965). Whenever a fight erupts among juveniles or adult females, the mere presence of a dominant male seems to be sufficient, in most instances, to restore order.

How do some males come to be dominant and others peripheral? To study this process, we must look at the socialization of a typical baboon. From birth until it is about one month old, the infant baboon clings to its mother's chest suckling, held by the mother. At this stage, the infant and mother are very attractive to other baboons, who groom the mother in an effort to get close to the baby. The mother usually stays close to the center of the troop and to the dominant males.

From one to about four months of age, the infant occasionally rides the mother's back, jockey-fashion. It stays almost constantly with the mother, although when it crawls close to other baboons, it finds them favorably disposed and tolerant. The infant and its mother still remain close to the dominant males in the center of the troop. From the fourth month until about a year, the infant gradually increases its contact with other young baboons, forming a play group in which mock fighting and chase establish a rank order of physical ability. Infants are weaned at about a year of age, spending part of their time with their mothers and part of their time with their peer group. In the young baboon's second year, the juvenile baboon, as it is now called, spends most of its time in the play group, turning for protection to the dominant males rather than to its mother or any other female.

In the third and fourth year of a baboon's life, almost all time is spent in the play group. By this time, the play has become very much rougher, and a hierarchy of dominance is beginning to emerge. Adults now act less charitably toward the young, and the juveniles are often chased by the dominant males. Females at this age leave the play group and join other females in grooming sessions. Grooming is that behavior often observed in zoos, where animals appear to be picking parasites out of each other's coat. Although no doubt some cleansing does occur, grooming behavior is more often a sign of social interaction. In a troop of baboons, all animals groom each other at different times. Females groom males, infants, juveniles, and each other. Males groom each other, females, and infants. Most grooming attention is given to the dominant males and to mothers of young infants.

From the fourth year until full maturity, the young males are considered subadults and remain among the peripheral males. With full maturity, young males which have established a relationship with one or more of the dominant males may move into the dominant hierarchy. Others remain peripheral. One male baboon, who was peripheral in his own troop, by fighting several dominant males in a neighboring troop became dominant in that troop (De Vore 1965:64). However, this is unusual behavior.

The dominant group is a fluctuating one, as older members lose agility and strength, they fall into the peripheral group. Their place of dominance is taken by one or more of the young adults, who then form their own alliances, bringing into the group young adults they favor and rejecting those they do not. Often, when a particular male drops out of the center of the group, his allies are also rejected from the dominance hierarchy. We can see that dominance is more a system of alliances than a matter of brute strength, although the weak and malformed are excluded from the hierarchy by their positions within the infant and juvenile play groups. It should be stressed that changes in the membership of the troop occur so seldom that few instances of it are recorded.

Among desert baboons there is a similar tendency for infants and females to be herded toward the rear while the males go forward to meet the enemy (Kummer, in Jay 1968). During movements of the band, the band travels in more compact formations than the savannah baboons. The main difference between the two types, in terms of social interaction, is the tendency of the desert baboon to form "two-man teams." This occurs when one male in a unit befriends a subadult male in his unit, and the two remain close to each other in the band, each herding his own females.

The savannah troop has strong biological bonds as well as social bonds. The estrous cycle of the female baboon runs about thirty-five days. Of this time, she is sexually responsive for about one week. During the early stages of the cycle, when genital swelling is minimal, dominant males will have no relations with the female, although she does present herself to them. At this stage, she usually has intercourse with the peripheral males. The dominant males do not interfere (Washburn 1961:97). For the few days of the maximal swelling, the female baboon forms a temporary consortship with a dominant male. Since the female is most fertile at this time, most of the progeny are the offspring of the dominant males. This probably accounts for the marked similarity in coat color in a given troop. With the genital swelling waning, the female is again open to the advances of the peripheral males. Although the female seldom goes into estrous while lactating, it does happen that a female with a young infant goes into her cycle. It is not unusual for the dominant males to "baby-sit" the infants while the mother goes the rounds with the peripheral males (De Vore 1965). This behavior does not occur with the desert baboon, where the female is closely herded. But even among these desert baboons, a juvenile female leaves her unit temporarily to copulate with a subadult male.

The group in this way satisfies all the needs of the individual: protection, social interaction, sexual gratification. Since baboons do not have free use of their hands, food is not shared or carried to other members of the troop. Even the young must forage for themselves when weaned. It is true that baboons can get along with a three-legged gait, and make rather good time, too, when carrying corn or bananas they have filched from some farmer's field. However, they can sustain this gait only for short intervals of time. Baboons cannot maintain a home place where infants can be cared for, the aged tended, and the ill recuperated. It is literally a matter of life and death that the individual baboon keep up with the troop as it ranges over its foraging area. Whereas a dominant male baboon will often fall back to escort a healthy female who has just given birth, the ill and the aged are given no such courtesy. Those who cannot keep up with the troop fall farther behind all the time and eventually are picked off by a cheetah or other predator. Among baboons, natural selection operates to keep the population confined largely to the strong and well.

One final point about baboons. There is much in popular literature about territoriality as pertains to man. There is no question but that territoriality exists among birds and many other species. A home range is delimited and defended. However, although each baboon troop has its own range, the ranges of different troops often overlap at some points. This is most frequently seen at watering places, where several baboon troops share the same water hole. No instances of fighting have been reported where such overlapping occurs (Washburn 1961:93). Smaller troops usually peacefully give way to larger troops. This is also seen in the day-to-day foraging process. Where troops converge upon the same locale, the smaller troop gives way to the larger one. There is also great tolerance between neighboring bands of the desert baboons. If there is such a quality as territoriality in human beings, then it probably does not derive from our primate heritage.

## Chimpanzees

Field studies of chimpanzees have been done by different groups of investigators, with some differences between their reports.

This may be due to the fact that different investigators observed different chimps, but it may also be due to differing interpretations. Where possible, both points of view will be given.

Chimpanzees are certainly the most entertaining of the great apes. We are strongly attracted to them, not only because of their antics, but because so many of their expressions, characteristics, and features bear strong resemblance to our own. Less visible characteristics also show the close relationship we share. For instance, cell antigens behave much the same way in chimpanzees as they do in man (Buettner-Janusch 1966:519–520). Red blood cells of chimpanzees react similarly to ours in response to certain proteins, and their ABO systems react much more like ours than like those of the orangutan. It remains to be seen whether this is indicative of a closer genetic relationship. Although these chemical similarities are intriguing, let us see what relationship, if any, exists between social behaviors.

Chimpanzees, like other great apes, walk on their hind legs and on the knuckles of their hands. Their specific adaptation is to *brachiation*—swinging from tree limbs. All indications are that our mutual ancestors, the Dryopithecines, were relatively unspecialized. We saw that Australopithecus gives evidence of adaptation to erect posture. It has been speculated that at about the same time as Ramapithecus, another form of the rapidly evolving Dryopithecines changed in the direction of the Pongidae, the great apes. At any rate, it should be remembered that the adaptation to brachiation was as profound as that to bipedalism, and probably took about the same length of time. Adaptation to tree-living necessitated longer arms, and, as a consequence, the ape on the ground walks primarily on the knuckles of his hands, the feet remaining unspecialized. Gibbons and orangutans are the apes most adapted to brachiation. Chimpanzees show a compromise adaptation, since they divide their time between trees and the ground. In their native forest, chimpanzees nest in trees at night and swing from tree to tree when traveling. At other times, they hunt food on the ground and spend much time on the ground in social interaction and slow travel.

The ape's environment proves ideal for its specific adaptations. The chimpanzee, for example, unlike the baboon, faces no known predator (Reynolds and Reynolds, in De Vore 1965:388). There is no need for the comparatively rigid social structuring of the baboon troop. And, indeed, the chimpanzee social unit is so unstructured that, despite years of field studies, we do not yet know how many chimpanzees consider themselves part of any particular group. They seem most casual in their bonds, two or three traveling together for some time, then parting company to take up with other companions. On the other hand, their communication network is wide. On occasions when groups of chimpanzees move to new food areas, they stamp on tree trunks, howl, and generally make a great deal of noise, thus alerting other groups that they are on the move (Goodall; Reynolds; in De Vore 1965). Other groups tend to go toward the sounds rather than away from them. Individuals are always combining in small groups, in larger clusters and in relatively large groups, only to break down again into pairs, trios, and other groups. The groups tend to be smaller and more widely scattered when food is scarce, and larger and denser in areas where fruit is plentiful (Reynolds and Reynolds, in De Vore 1965:409). The only stable unit in chimpanzee society seems to be the mother-child relationship. Even after young chimpanzees have grown, they tend to make their nightly nests near their mothers.

When we dealt with baboon population, we could neatly give the approximate number of individuals in the troop and the area they inhabited. But one field investigator found it impossible to make an accurate count of the chimpanzee population in a particular reserve, partly because the apes were not restricted to the reserve, and partly because of the difficulty of recognizing all individuals encountered (Goodall, in De Vore 1965:430). She goes on to estimate the chimpanzee population as about eighty individuals in the thirty square miles of the reserve, estimating the density as 3.3 chimps per square mile.

Chimpanzees are largely fruit eaters, although they also eat many other plants and insects and hunt meat. For example, a pair of hunting chimpanzees killed a monkey they saw up in a tree. The first chimpanzee climbed a neighboring tree, while the monkey watched it, fascinated. While the monkey was so absorbed, the second chimp climbed up behind it, and broke its neck, the two chimps sharing the kill (Van Lawick-Goodall 1968).

An even more remarkable trait that chimps display is also connected with food-getting. Chimpanzees have been seen making tools of vine, grass, or twigs to insert into termite holes. After a moment the chimp removes the tool, which now has termites hanging on to it, licks off the termites and reinserts it. We call these *tools* because the vines, twigs, or grasses are deliberately selected to be no more than twelve inches long. Vines and twigs are shorn of their leaves before use. When a vine or twig end is broken, the chimp either breaks that end off, or turns the twig around and uses the other end. One male chimp found the termite hole too deep for his piece of grass; he looked about and went some distance away to pick a longer piece of vine. Individuals also seem to have preferences about the material they use, some preferring twigs, others vines or grasses.

Chimpanzees go through infant and juvenile stages very much like those of the baboon. From one to six months, the infant is totally dependent on its mother and never out of her sight. From six months to about two years of age, the infant still suckles, but this gradually tapers off and solid food is taken. Time spent with the mother becomes gradually less, although even as a juvenile, at the age of seven or eight, a chimpanzee will keep close contact with its mother. This is followed by adolescence from the ages of seven to ten years. By age ten or eleven, chimpanzees are fully mature, and their maximum age is somewhere around thirty years. Nowhere is there mention of the juvenile or infant play groups so important to baboon social organization. Young chimps play together, of course, but this is done in another context. Where mothers gather together, their children play together. When the mother changes her associations, so does the juvenile.

That chimpanzees learn readily is evident to all of us who have been entertained by trained chimpanzees. In the wild, much learned behavior is also apparent. Nest-building, for example, is evidently learned by chimpanzees when they are infants. They observe their mother making a nest and then they go off and make "play" nests of their own.

The chimpanzee female also has an estrous cycle similar to the baboon's, averaging thirty-five days, with a peak of fertility about a week in mid-cycle. Copulation among chimpanzees appears to be more random than among baboons. Either the male or the female may initiate the courtship, and mating takes place as a result of proximity or individual choice rather than through a dominance pattern.

And now we come to the only point where the main investigators (Goodall; Reynolds and Reynolds) appear to disagree. Although Goodall states that aggressive and submissive interactions between individuals are rare because of the loose social structuring, she does see some dominance interaction between individuals (in De Vore 1965:453). On the other hand, Reynolds and Reynolds (in De Vore 1965:415) do not see dominance behavior manifest in chimpanzee bands. In fact, they view chimpanzee bands as fluid and constantly changing in numbers and composition, bands often being composed only of males or only of females. When we examine more closely what Goodall tentatively calls dominance behavior, we note that it is situational and individual, having no bearing on the welfare of the troop as a whole. For example, several chimpanzees ran away screaming when approached by an angry male. But this may show more prudence than dominance. And when two chimpanzees want the same piece of fruit, they do not fight, for one normally gives way to the other (Goodall, in De Vore 1965:453). Nothing reported resembles the tightly integrated dominance clique of baboons, with its protective and order-keeping functions.

If chimpanzees are so superbly adapted, and live under such idyllic conditions, we wonder what limits their population growth. The answer appears to be the periodic famines caused by blight or failures of fruit crops, and the progressive narrowing of their forests as man puts more and more land under cultivation. The tragic story of man's incursions into the domain of the great apes is told in *The Year of the Gorilla* (Schaller 1964), in which we view a dying species, apathetically existing in the last bit of what probably was once a mighty range. Too apathetic to do more than eat and sleep, gorillas are failing to reproduce themselves in the wild. Fortunately, the chimpanzee has not reached this pass, and with the setting up of game reserves, he may indeed be spared.

### Chimpanzee Communication

An enormous amount of data has been collected concerning chimpanzee communication. As many as twenty-three types of cries and calls are used by the chimpanzee (Goodall, in De Vore 1965:462–464). That these vocalizations are signals to other chimpanzees is implicit in the data, which note not only the conditions under which each call is given, but also what the response was from other chimpanzees. The level of symbolizing a chimpanzee can vocally attain is less than that achieved by man's use of language. For example, if a chimpanzee emits what Goodall calls "a quiet high-pitched 'hu,'" a chimpanzee looks at the caller, and then looks around to see the reason for the call. In other words, the chimpanzee who originally calls cannot transmit information regarding the reason for the call. The difference between this and human language is the difference between, "Look out," and, "Look out, there is a predator on the left."

 In addition to vocalizations, chimpanzees employ a wide range of gestures in such contexts that they must have specific meanings. Several gestures used by the chimps are quite familiar to us from our own repertoire. For example, upon meeting an unknown chimpanzee, a chimp will extend his arm, palm up, and touch the unfamiliar chimp on the head, shoulders, and groin. This extension of the hand, so familiar to us in the handshake, seems to have a broad use in the primate world. The same can be said for the greeting hug given by chimpanzees who know each other. This resembles nothing so much as the typical Latin American *embrazzo*. Jumping up and down and hooting when excited are gestures humans also use. And who, in the presence of a small child, has not at some time squatted to the ground and extended his arms, the response typically being that the child runs into the embrace. The very same gesture and response are used among chimpanzees.

In captivity, chimps have been trained to do many acrobatic tricks, some of which require a great deal of physical coordination—performing on bicycles, on roller skates, and the like. There have also been several attempts to teach chimpanzees to communicate with human beings.

A husband-and-wife team worked with a chimpanzee named Viki (Hayes and Hayes 1951). They attempted to teach Viki to speak. In six years, Viki only learned four sounds which could be interpreted as words.

Another man-and-wife team, recognizing that chimpanzees in the wild use gestures as a means of communication at least as much as vocalization, decided to try to communicate with Washoe, an infant chimpanzee, in the sign language used by the deaf (Gardner and Gardner 1969). At the end of twenty-two months, Washoe had learned thirty signs. Washoe began to combine several signs into meaningful statements and questions as soon as she had learned eight or ten different signs, and the signs used did not remain specific to particular objects but were generalized to a wide class of appropriate objects. This is characteristic of the way man uses language.

Perhaps the most exciting experiment of this nature has been with a chimpanzee named Sarah (Premack and Premack 1972). The investigators used colored plastic symbols of varying shapes. Each piece of plastic represented a word. Sarah learned 130 words. She not only demonstrated her ability to read the words by obeying commands stated in the plastic shapes, but she also showed the ability to create sentences and ask questions. It is apparent that Sarah's comprehension of language as a form of communication is quite comparable to that of a young child. In one incident, Sarah, using her plastic symbols, wrote the sentence, "Give apple Gussie." Gussie is the name of another chimpanzee. The trainer gave Gussie an apple. Sarah never repeated the sentence.

Unquestionably, man has long underestimated the abilities of other primates to symbolize. But it remains to be seen whether chimpanzees who have been taught a sign language can communicate with each other using that language without the intervention of a human being (Hewes 1973:6). And will a trained chimpanzee be able to teach its knowledge to its offspring?

Desmond Morris (1962), who is also the author of *The Naked Ape,* did some very interesting work with chimpanzees in a zoo. He provided them with finger-painting material and allowed them to paint. He found that several patterns emerged. The chimps engaged first in general sweeping motions, never going out of the bounds of the paper. They then learned that a different design could be made by using the tips of their fingers to make small round designs. The frequently combined both designs. After some time, the chimpanzees created a fan-like design by placing their fingers flat upon the paper. This design proved the ultimate innovation in finger-painting. Morris was able to continue his experiment by giving the chimps drawing pads and charcoal pencils. Whereas at first the animals used the same type of sweeping strokes they had used in painting, they soon learned to make smaller, more geometric designs which were illustrative of better control of the new medium. Although Morris continued the experiments, the chimpanzees never went beyond drawing small geometric designs. They never attempted to represent an actual object.

Morris compares this behavior with that of nurseryschool children given charcoal and paper. Nurseryschool children at first lacked the fine coordination of the chimps, and their sweeps went off the margins of the paper regularly. It took children a longer time to acquire the precision needed to make the geometric designs, but quickly after acquiring that skill they went on to draw representations of objects in their world, something the chimps never did.

It would seem, then, that chimpanzees start from a base similar to man: they think, make tools, communicate, and socialize. However, man has been able to elaborate upon these skills and build a complex symbolic culture, whereas monkeys and apes fail to go beyond a certain degree of elaboration. It is for this reason that we term the social behavior of apes and monkeys *proto-culture* or *pre-culture,* to distinguish it from the highly evolved and symbolic culture of man.

# CHAPTER 5

# What Color
# Are Colored People?

A new young secretary, who was also militantly black, was told by some of her co-workers to guard her purse, because the office was prey to a pair of purse snatchers. They were described as young and wearing dungarees; one was bearded, and the other was colored. The young lady briskly asked, "What color is he?"

Indeed, this is a question we all might ask. Does the individual we are referring to conform to a racial stereotype, or is he just someone whose skin shade is different from ours? Non-anthropological literature is a veritable jungle of phrases like the "English race" and the "Jewish race." People who have English nationality encompass many religions and races. People who profess the Jewish faith are of many nationalities and races. *Race* is a term that has not been defined so as to satisfy all scientists concerned with it. But the term has been much abused in our century. In fact, some anthropologists decline to use the word, claiming it is a social construct, rather than a biological entity.

This would seem especially true when we regard two examples. The first is from our own society. A child with a black parent and a white parent is always considered black, or Negro, or colored. Actually no more than half his genes are drawn from a black gene pool, so why don't we accentuate his Caucasian inheritance? Another example comes from Brazil, where there are many more descriptive phrases having to do with color, including *café-au-lait, negre, blanco,* and several more. But the unusual factor is that these terms are not based on skin color alone. They have to do with education, wealth, and status. An ethnologist who worked in South America reports that a black engineer, in a small Brazilian town, was considered a *blanco* ("white"), whereas a Caucasian drunkard was spoken of as *negre* ("black") (Wagley 1963:142–143).

Despite the obvious confusion, most of us think in terms of stereotypes when we think of race. And if we were to look at populations more closely, we would discover, within each so-called race, a great deal of variety. We think we know what we mean when we speak about race, but do we really?

## Defining Race

In order to clarify the concept of race, let us differentiate two aspects of race and define them.

Race can be spoken of as a biological entity, a differentiation of gene frequencies between breeding populations. Let us take eye-color as an example. There are blue-eyed or grey-eyed people in both the "black race" and the "white race." However, there are many more blue- or grey-eyed people among whites. So, what we are speaking of is not lack of eye-color altogether, nor an eye-color like orange that is peculiar to only one population, namely whites. When talking about racial type, we are talking about the frequency with which brown eyes or blue eyes appear.

The biological entity of race, as defined above, must not be confused with species. A *species* is generally regarded as a population that does not normally interbreed with other populations, and, when such breeding is induced, the offspring are sterile. The horse is a different species from the donkey, because when they are interbred, the mule, which results, is sterile. All races of man are capable of interbreeding and producing fertile offspring. We shall give some examples later.

We must also never confuse race, as a factor of biology, with racism. *Racism* is the attribution of cultural characteristics to physical types. There is no basis in fact for racism, because members of all races can be encultured into differing cultures. Race is inherited. Culture is learned.

## The Biology of Race

Let us first discuss the biological concept of race. Race is a matter of gene frequencies, as shown in the eye-color example. Membership in a racial group is inherited. Heredity is controlled by the molecule deoxyribonucleic acid (DNA). DNA is stored in chromosomes in the nucleus of each cell. The egg and the sperm cell each has half the number of chromosomes present in the resulting embryo cell. Upon fertilization, the fetus receives half of its chromosomes from each parent, making up the full complement of forty-six chromosomes. Each chromosome is made up of segments that are responsible for the production of a complete protein molecule. These segments are called *genes*.

The genes interact with both the internal and the external environment to produce the characteristics of the new individual. The chemical action of some genes inhibit the action of other genes, so that we speak of a *genotype*, meaning the actual genes an individual has, and a *phenotype*, the appearance of the individual. For example, if the gene for brown eyes completely inhibited the action of the gene for blue eyes, a person who actually had one gene for blue eyes and one for brown would appear brown-eyed, phenotypically. (In actuality, such a person would more likely have hazel or grey eyes, since the chemical reaction may not be complete.) For each reaction of a gene, there are alternative reactions, which are called *alleles*. Eyes can be blue, grey, green, hazel or brown. These colors are all alleles of eye-color—different chemical reactions in the same gene.

Variety is introduced into a gene pool by mutation, or by linkage or breakage of chromosomes, as well as by the randomness of the sample from the gene pool out of which the individual is born.

Two factors about human genetics must be stressed. First, many of our characteristics depend on the combination of several genes working together. Skin color is an example of this. The shade of one's skin depends on the presence of dark granules, called *melanin*, which occur in cells called melanocytes. The relative darkness or lightness of a person's skin depends on the number of genes acting for greater melanin concentration in that particular individual. The second factor is that the action of a single gene may influence several characteristics.

Individuals do not evolve, but populations do. A *Mendelian population*, that is, a reproductive community of individuals who share a common gene pool (Buettner-Janusch 1966:633), normally contains a variety of phenotypes. Through the action of natural selection, certain phenotypes will have an adaptive advantage to a particular environment. As the population expands in that area, a maximal density places a strain upon food resources, and groups split off into new environments. These new populations, temporarily cut off from the parent colony, form a different gene pool. Through the continuing action of mutation, reassortment, recombination, and the adaptive stresses of the new environment, the new population may become phenotypically quite distinct from the parent population.

Especially in small populations, such factors as *genetic drift* may be important. This refers to the fact that the original founders of a new colony themselves embody only a few of the many variations in the original gene pool, and it is these few variations which form the basis of the new colony. These conditions existed in man's early history, and, as we shall see, they continue in modified form into the present. It is probable that early man had many Mendelian populations exhibiting shifts in gene frequencies. However, it should be noted that "populations may diverge from one another at one point in time, but they may merge again later" (Alland 1971:21). For this reason, the definition of race as an ephemeral evolutionary episode (Hulse 1963: 369) is particularly apt. The races of man are not and have never been species. Interbreeding, merging, separation of populations have gone on all through man's history and are still going on.

The popular concept of race is woefully inadequate. The phenotypic expressions we regard as indicative of race are such things as skin color, eye shape, hair texture. Making the same error that the classifiers of fossil man did, an archetype was created, popularly called a stereotype. Individuals are ranked on the scale of race according to how closely they approach this archetype. What do you do with individuals who have the "right" skin color but the "wrong" hair texture? Much more significant traits, such as blood groupings, which may indeed have adaptive significance, are not considered at all in popular concepts. We do not distinguish between individuals who have different body chemistries, but we do distinguish those who have a slightly different skin color. We should keep in mind that an individual is not the population, and within the total population called a race, many variations in skin color and other traits will appear. In fact, it is unquestioned that there is a significant overlap in such traits as skin color between so-called races. There are many individuals classified as "black" who are of considerably lighter skin tone than some darker individuals we classify as "white."

In popular parlance, we are accustomed to thinking in terms of four major races: white, red, yellow, and black. These leave us with whole populations that do not fit any of the neat pigeon-holes. What are we to do with the Bushman of the Kalahari Desert in Africa, who is brownish-orange in color and has freckles? And where do we put the Australian aborigine who is quite black, but has other distinctive features? Do we assume the

Pygmies of Oceania are of the same "race" as the Pygmies of Africa? If we do, we are mistaken, because their blood groupings are much closer to Asiatic ones, whereas those of the African pygmy closely resemble African blood groups. And we classify the Basques of Europe as Caucasian, yet they have a much higher percentage of Rh negative blood than any other group in Europe, and an Rh positive woman would have a great deal of trouble bearing a live child if her husband were a Basque.

Race is a classificatory term. Races are distinguished in order to test shifts in genetic frequencies. What constitutes a race depends upon the problem for which the classification was devised. If that problem concerns blood groupings, there will be many more than four races distinguishable. The same is true if we speak of geographical races, and seldom will these two ways of classifying race overlap. It is true, however, that certain populations can be distinguished from others. There are shifts in gene frequencies among populations based upon the merging of populations and the separation of others. Among the facts that emerge from a knowledge of man's evolution and his history is the fact that there never was a "pure" race, and there never will be.

Within the last four hundred years, at least two new races have been formed out of the merging of separate Mendelian populations. One is the American black, who can trace fully a fifth of his ancestry to Caucasian ancestors, the other four-fifths or so being distinctively West African black, as opposed to East or South African black, all of whose populations show distinctive shifts in gene frequencies. The other race is mestizo, the product of the merging of people who are primarily Mediterranean Caucasian Spaniard with American Indians. There are also some minor "races" formed by the population migrations set into motion by technological improvements in communication. Fisher (1913) for example, studied an isolated population in South Africa who kept records of their genealogies going back to the founders of the colony. These founders were Dutch Boers, who took Hottentot (a native South African group) wives. They set up a village in an isolated valley, where the women were quickly converted to Christianity and European dress, and their descendants proved a charming admixture of Hottentot and Boer traits. Another such fascinating mixture occurred between the sailors of the ship *Bounty*, the famed mutineers, and the Tahitian women they took off to Pitcairn Island. In this case, too, the men imposed European ways upon their wives. The descendants of this group have such a record of longevity and good health that they have been described as possessing "hybrid vigor" (Shapiro 1929).

Even as some populations are merging, others are being segregated. Cultural factors now play a larger part than previously in the creation of breeding populations. Matings are not random, but rather selective for matters of religion, race, social standing, education, and even nationality. Thus, imperceptibly, race and culture interact.

Race, used biologically, must be seen as evidence of variety in human populations. Since this is one of the prerequisites to survival as a species, to say nothing of evolution, variety is highly desirable. Science is far from being able to predict, let alone control, all the selective cultural and natural pressures involved in the evolution of man. For this reason, it is dangerous to impose hypothetical limits on the variability of man. Science fiction notions, like the replication of an "ideal" type, would imperil the survival of the species. Suppose your ideal was not immune to some virus that has not yet been formed? In the natural course of events, variability among individuals and among breeding populations are likely to remain with us. What do we do with this variability culturally?

Donoghue (1963:1000) gives us this list of characteristics of a minority group, as seen by the majority: they are dirty, barbarous, dangerous, criminal, irresponsible, diseased, have distorted sex organs, and intermarriage with them produces diseased children. This stereotype so pervades our own culture that it comes as a shock to us to read that this is how the Japanese think of the people who used to be called the Eta (now the Burakamine). The Eta were supposedly the vestiges of a Caucasian population which had settled in Japan prior to occupation by the Orientals. In fact, the objective observer notices few racial differences between the native Japanese and the Eta, though the social gap is wide.

Despite all cultural attempts to prevent interbreeding, most minority groups exhibit evidence of considerable intermingling with the majority group. The American black is an example of this, as is the Jew, who in India resembles Indians, in Ethiopia resembles Ethiopians, and so forth. The ideas prevalent in a given culture about race can be, at times, quite ludicrous. For example, Hitler spoke a great deal about the Aryan race, who were to become masters of the world. "Aryan" is not a biological category but a linguistic one. The only Aryan-speaking people present in Germany during Hitler's time were the gypsies, whom he condemned to the gas chambers. In our time, the polemics about race have hit hysterical proportions, and little can be added to the great amount that has already been stated, written, and argued. The greatest dangers, however, lie not in the blatantly ignorant racists, but in two other forms: the subtle type of racist that hides behind greater issues, and the new "scientific" racism.

## Racism in America

Housing and busing have been two issues of the first type. In North and South, in urban and rural area, the outcry against busing has been profound. It is cloaked as worry about the welfare of small children who must travel by bus to their schools. It was only a generation ago that parents were boasting of how they walked miles through rain and snow in order to get to school. Buses would have been considered almost sinful luxury in those days. Moreover, in rural areas where there is no significant black population, consolidated schools centrally located, where all children must be bused to the campus, have been the rule for years. Why the hue and cry now? Obviously, the present outcry is due to the fact that now children are being bused to integrated schools. That racism pervades our society is obvious when we map the areas of busing protests. The North was quiet while the South was in turmoil because the southern schools were being integrated. When integration spread to the northern cities, the outcry came from that direction. The well-to-do suburbs, with few exceptions, joined the fracas when integration threatened their schools. White parents cry out in dismay because their children ride past perfectly good "neighborhood" schools to get to more distant integrated schools. This is supposedly detrimental to the health and well-being of their children. Where were they when black children were being bused past their perfectly good neighborhood schools to the all-black school?

The tragedy in this situation is that many valid issues are lost in the intensity of emotion. Certainly "quality education for all" is a desirable goal, but when used as a slogan by overt racists, it becomes suspect. Certainly, neighborhood schools are desirable, but how, then, will we integrate the neighborhoods? Black teachers and students, too, have valid objections to the new integration policies. Black teachers, many of whom were trained in inadequate and segregated schools, are fearful that they cannot compete successfully with the better trained white teachers. Black students who were leaders in the activities of their segregated schools fear competition for leadership positions from more articulate whites. Many black parents have come to realize that white teachers do not understand black ghetto children.

Despite the validity of all these factors, unless we are to continue to evolve two separate cultures, each potentially lethal to the other, a break with the old system must be made. Whenever that break is made, the generations alive at that time will have to undergo some painful adaptations. The cry, "Why me?" is as old as Job. The only thing that can ease the pain of this type of adaptation is fuller knowledge and understanding of the peoples involved, and of the objectives to be attained.

The issue of busing is racism cloaked in emotion. The issue of housing is racism cloaked in economics. Restricting a portion of the population to a ghetto area is one way of substantially increasing the income from substandard housing. People are forced to pay a great deal of rent a month for housing which would, under normal conditions, be unrentable. There is no need to improve the housing because no matter how bad the condition, there is a ready market. Unscrupulous "block-busters" force the naive and credulous out of fringe areas, so that the buildings can be rented to blacks or other minorities at a considerable increase in rents.

Economics also governs the sale of homes in suburbs. An area of small low-cost homes is ripe for the unscrupulous realtor who panics the neighborhood by selling a house to a black. He then buys the other houses cheaply, reselling them to blacks at a premium. The terror spread is very real. Often, these small homes represent the life-savings of a small wage-worker who hasn't the capital to invest in another home. The tragedy here is that the rightful anger felt by the small home-owner is not directed toward the realtor but rather toward the other victims, the blacks.

A few neighborhoods have refused to panic in such situations and have become peacefully integrated. Laurelton, in Queens, is an example of a community actively combatting real estate interests. But in the same borough of New York, the threat of a low-cost housing project to be built in a predominantly middle-class white neighborhood caused a storm of protest which did much to kill the presidential aspirations of New York's mayor. Were it not for the stereotype of the criminal, dirty, and diseased minority group, there would scarcely be reason for the panic. Sales of houses take place routinely without emotional furor in the neighborhood. Low-cost housing is not in and of itself offensive. Private interests have built and rented units of varying prices back to back all over the country. It is the stigma of the black that haunts white America.

Still another area fraught with ambiguity is the equal job opportunity question. One cannot fully appreciate the irony that racism causes unless one looks at the situation in many unions today. It was only a short time ago that the union movement was in the forefront of progressive social change. Many present union leaders can recall the turn of the century, when pitched battles were fought between labor and management for minimally humane working conditions. How strange to see those same leaders today refusing entrance into the apprentice training programs of their unions to all but a few token blacks. Unions, since the early 1940s, have become big business. They have special interests to protect, namely, jobs for their people. Today, many craft workers and workers in large industrial plants feel threatened by automation. Their skills are such that they cannot easily be retrained. Opening the union to blacks simply creates a larger labor force to compete for fewer jobs.

One occasionally hears someone state that he cannot understand why blacks did not integrate themselves into American society like so many other groups did: the Italians, the Jews, the Irish. The answer is not only the factor of the high visibility of blacks, but also the fact that the other immigrant groups came to the United States during a time of an expanding labor need. The Irish came in time to build railroads, the Jews to man small factories. The blacks were brought here by force to man cotton plantations. The cotton plantation worked by hand is today as obsolete as the dinosaur, and blacks have entered the labor market at the very time the market is contracting in size. Because of the special conditions and attitudes of slavery, no attempt was made to help the rural, agrarian black to become an urban, industrial worker. Thus he remains, long after the absorption of other groups, the stranger in our midst.

*Xenophobia,* fear of strangers, is common to many peoples of the world. As with any other fear, it can be conquered through facing it, and becoming familiar with the object of our fear, so that in time the feared object loses its strangeness. Possibly this could happen in our society were it not for politicians who inflame these fears for their own purposes, and for the proponents of "scientific" racism. Politicians are not often taken seriously, and their motives are suspect even to the most naive citizens. But intellectuals, philosophers, and professionals are commonly regarded as disinterested purveyors of fact, and their statements are taken seriously.

Unfortunately, the work of such social scientists as Jensen can easily lend itself to interpretation as an affirmation of racism. Jensen is an educational psychologist whose article "How Much Can We Boost I.Q. and Scholastic Achievement?" appeared in the *Harvard Educational Review* in 1969 and caused a furor among people interested in education. Briefly stated, Jensen's position is that black children score consistently lower on IQ tests than their white peers, and they consistently underachieve in class. Jensen attributes this to hereditary factors, and he leans heavily on statistics, which few people can fathom, to making the report more "scientific." It may be that the report received so much publicity because it gave a "scientific" accreditation to something that both educators and the public were noticing, the relatively poor academic performance of many black children. Many papers were written and presented by social scientists refuting Jensen's analysis and interpretation of the data. But, unfortunately, these refutations made little impact on the general public. Perhaps this was because, in the experience of both teachers and parents, segments of the black population do poorly academically, and it was nice to know that it was a racial characteristic and thus could not be altered.

In an earlier chapter we discussed enculturation and acculturation. We said that children are informally encultured, from birth, in the mores and values of their culture. We also said that human beings from one culture could and did become accultured to a different culture. Let us now examine Jensen's theory in this light.

We will start by observing that there are different levels of academic achievement between white middle-class children and black ghetto children. We will also state that the black child is a member of a subculture that is within a larger culture represented by the middle-class white child. Intelligence testing, as currently used, is not at all a value-free instrument; that is, IQ tests are more a measure of a person's familiarity with middle-class Western culture than a true measure of "pure" intelligence (defined as the ability to recognize and cope with reality). An example of the culture-bound nature of IQ tests would be a question where a picture of a cup is shown and the child is asked to pair it with a table, a saucer, or another item. The middle-class white child chooses the saucer. The black ghetto child, never having seen a cup and saucer used at home, chooses the table and is marked wrong. In 1973 a Black Intelligence Test for Cultural Homogeneity was published in some local papers. Among the questions was one of definition. Several words were listed, and the phrase defining it most closely was to be chosen by the child. For example, is "apple alley" a brick, a piece of fruit, a dog, or a horse? The correct answer is a brick, but few white students would get that right.

The black subculture speaks a language of its own and has certain values that have survival value in that society.

One of the difficulties with the present educational system is something which might be called the "empty wastebasket concept." In this concept, the educator views the five- or six-year-old as an empty wastebasket. All the educator has to do is wad up little bits of knowledge and fill the wastebasket, and the child will leave the school an educated middle-class American. This does not work. By the time a child gets to school, he is already a fairly well encultured member of his society. If his society is white and middle class, he has easy sailing, no value conflicts, and will be able to accept the "facts" given him, and will do well academically. If, however, his society is poor and black, the "facts" will seem irrelevant or downright preposterous, and the values taught would probably get him killed the first day he tried them on his block. He probably must make the choice whether to do well academically or survive.

Let us take the little ditty most of us learned as small children—something to the effect that "the policeman is your friend, a helping hand he will lend." The advice given in the ditty—ask the policeman when you are lost or in trouble—is absolute nonsense to the child whose father and older brothers are terrorized by police. What can a child who has never sat down to a balanced dinner make of Dick and Jane and their well-ordered home? What can he make of the constant admonitions not to fight when he must fight to survive in his neighborhood? And what of the trips to parks, zoos, and beaches when this child's life is bounded by cement pavements and gang rivalries? The cultural gap between the two worlds of America is huge, so that members of different subcultures cannot even understand each other's symbolism. Southern white high school students fight desperately to continue to use the Confederate flag and the song "Dixie" as their school symbols after the schools are integrated. They cannot understand black objections because, as they say, "It's only a song." They do not understand this symbolism until you ask them why they don't substitute "Marching Through Georgia," a song that symbolizes the burning that accompanied General Sherman's "March to the Sea" in the Civil War.

The black child, in sum, enters school bearing a different culture, speaking a different language. No attempts are made by the schools to acculture a black as they would a child of a different nationality. No allowances are made for the black's linguistic differences. Educators fail to do this not because they are unkind. Teachers will take extraordinary pains to help a child obviously recently arrived from another nation. But they fail to do this because they do not recognize that the black child, too, has arrived from another land, in effect, and he must return to that land when school is out. They do not perceive the reality of the cultural differences, which they so readily perceive in other nationalities.

There are other reasons why the black child often fails in the academic world. We are just beginning to understand the effects of malnutrition or of the mother's poor nutrition while she is pregnant. Studies have shown that protein deficiency can interfere with mental development in the unborn. Chronic malnutrition among blacks is the rule, not the exception.

There are, therefore, many reasons for differential school performance between white middle-class children and black poor children. Several questions must be answered before we can accept the thesis that such differences are racially inherited. One should compare the test scores of white students from Appalachia, a poor area, with test scores of white students from more affluent areas. Ideally, one should compare the test scores of students from Appalachia who have moved to large cities, such as Detroit, with the test scores of white middle-class students native to Detroit.

Additionally, data should be collected to compare the performance of children whose mothers had poor nutrition while pregnant with those whose mothers were adequately nourished. For this it is not necessary to use data collected in poverty areas. There are many instances of white middle-class mothers who consistently eat protein-poor food, either from choice or from extremes of climate or illness. Sociologists have long shown that the educational level of the home is important in determining the IQ of the child. Children from homes where reading and discussion are important tend to do better on IQ tests than children from other types of homes. Long ago, anthropologists studied twins who were separated at birth and adopted into different families. It was found that the children who were adopted into the homes of teachers, ministers, and professional people who read and were articulate scored higher on IQ tests than their twins who were adopted by farmers, storekeepers, and other people who did not place such a high value on reading and discussion.

After we have gathered all relevant data, and when it is weighed, we should recall that while white the ethnic groups were being aided by settlement houses and social workers to attend schools, even at night, if necessary, black children were being forcibly kept out of school.

# CHAPTER 6

# In the Word
# Was the Beginning

As an erect, bipedal primate, man has domesticated himself through his unique adaptation: culture. Culture is based, to a large extent, upon man's ability to symbolize. Nowhere is this ability exemplified better than in language.

Animals have systems of communication. Bees dance, some animals emit odors, others have more evolved systems of communication. Primate communication involves both sound and gesture. This is more highly developed than a system using cries alone. We might even say that communication "evolves" from systems that use cries alone to systems that combine cries and gestures, then to man's own use of language.

With man, communication has expanded into a number of channels. Oral language has been supplemented by written language. Written language has now been augmented by electronic systems which enable us to see and hear events taking place at a distance. In time, no doubt, simultaneous aural and visual exchanges will take place over distances now impossible for us to manage.

Through the accumulation of small changes, communication has evolved from a system capable of expressing merely a generalized cry to those within auditory distance to a system whereby we can see and hear from our livingrooms the great events of the world as they take place. When a chimpanzee utters a cry, another chimpanzee looks up and then looks around to see what event provoked the cry. There is a vast difference between this kind of communication and the ability to understand complex conceptualizations referring to abstractions we can neither see nor hear nor feel. Understanding a lecture on poetry would be impossible for a chimpanzee, and patriotic speeches would be wasted, as well. The quantum leap between communication signs and gestures and language as employed by man is in man's ability to symbolize. The ability to speak and to think in abstractions, the ability to convey an image of things which occurred in the past, or which may occur in the future, an ability to convey impressions only subjectively felt—these are unique to man.

### History of Language

Unfortunately, oral language leaves no physical remains for the archaeologist to analyze, so we cannot state with certainty when man's use of language began. Undoubtedly, man was equipped with the ability to make gestures and cries from the start, but we cannot state with precision when his ability to communicate abstractions started. Indirect evidence, as we shall show in the following chapters, indicates this may have been possible during the stage we have called Homo erectus. There appears to be evidence that at that time men shared some customs which could have been conveyed to each other only through the use of language. Certainly, by the time we approach the Neanderthal stage, shared value systems and beliefs existed that imply a fully developed use of language—a far cry indeed from the grunts and shrugs cartoonists have led us to believe were the speech patterns not only of Neanderthal but of the modern Indian!

Although we cannot say precisely when language as we know it began, we can define language, and perhaps thus clarify its features. *Language* is a system of symbols, combined according to certain rules which may vary from language to language but which are consistent within any one language. Language is the system whereby meanings and sounds are correlated through the mechanism of *syntax,* or structure of separate language elements.

### Structure of Language

*Phonemes* are the smallest classes of sound in a language. These sound units do not each have a meaning. They are merely sounds. Although one may think that the letters of our alphabet correspond with phonemes, they do not do so exactly, because we have several sounds which need two or more letters of the alphabet to express, such as *ch, sh,* or *tz.* Some letters can represent more than one phoneme. The letter *p,* for example, explodes with a burst of air in the word *pin.* In the word *spin,* however, no such burst of air accompanies the sound.

At this point, it might be worth noting that the sounds we use are not the only possible sounds. Speakers of the Khoisan languages, found in Africa, use a series of clicks made by the tongue against the roof of the mouth. The varieties of ways various languages use the *r* sound constitute phonemes. The Spanish-speaker's soft, rolled *n,* as in *mañana,* is a phoneme, whereas our plain *n,* as in *bin,* is a different phoneme.

Phonemes, in every language, are combined to form morphemes. *Morphemes* are the smallest units of meaning in a language, although they do not necessarily constitute words. In English, for example, *-ing* is a morpheme meaning "in the act of," and *-s* or *-es* are common English morphemes meaning "more than one" (plural ending).

Phonemes combine into morphemes, and morphemes are combined into words. Words are combined according to rules that are consistent within a given language. These rules are called *grammar.*

One of the basic points about language is the fact that the symbols used are completely arbitrary. As Shakespeare said long ago, "A rose by any other name would smell as sweet." There is nothing in the combination of sounds *r-o-s-e* that in any way resembles a rose, and if it were not that speakers of English have agreed that a rose is a *rose,* a rose could very well be called a *petunia.* The word *rose* is an excellent example of the symbolic use of language, because, in reading only the word *rose,* you would have to know the context before you could decide whether the combination of letters meant "flower" or "did rise."

Another principle of language is that its expansive capacity is nearly infinite. New words can be created, and phonemes and morphemes can be combined to form new expressions. This is often shown in learning a language. Often, the bright sayings of children involve a play on words inherent in experimenting with the ways of recombining phonemes and morphemes and applying the rules of grammar, such as the child who, on being told to behave, replied, "I am being have." He had grasped the grammatical concept of the verb *to be* but was confused by the use of the syllable *have* and thus created a new noun.

## Language Change

This is one way languages change. As anyone who owns an old dictionary can tell you, languages do change through time. They may change through the addition of words. Sometimes new words are created out of morphemes to mean something new in that society. The words *television* and *automobile* are such additions. When television and automobiles were invented, it was also necessary to invent names for them. These names were created out of syllables having specific meanings: *tele*, "distant" plus *vision*, "to see" equals *television*, "to see from a distance." *Auto*, "self" plus *mobile*, "moving" equals "self-propelling."

Words may also be borrowed from other languages. One may come to understand not only the historic contacts of a society through its language, but also the nature of those contacts. The English language has many borrowed words. Some are nouns, such as *squaw, tepee, algebra, pariah, bamboo*. These illustrate the far-flung connections of English-speakers. Other borrowed words tell us more about the nature of these connections. For example, *cattle, cow*, and *bull* are Anglo-Saxon in origin. However, when these meats come to the table they are in the form of *beef* or *veal*, words of French derivation. Even if we did not know historically of the Norman conquest of England, we should guess the outcome of that war by knowing, through words, who grew the cattle and who ate the beef.

Other connections are found to be more deeply rooted in the language. The English *good, better, best* series is directly related to the Germanic *gut, besser, beste*. We should guess at a genetic relationship here, and, indeed, linguists tell us that English and German are derived from a common ancestral language.

Just as languages change through the adoption of new words, they also change through obsolescence of other words. The familiar conjugation *thou shalt*, for example, has become archaic in English and is now only used by certain religious sects and in Biblical prose. Often, ritualized procedures, such as in churches or courtrooms, preserve archaic forms of speech no longer in common usage.

One of the most common ways a language changes is through the formation of dialects. When speakers of a common language separate from each other, each group develops certain speech patterns which may differ from the shared language. These differences come about in various ways, sometimes through variations in pronunciation that become an accepted pattern, sometimes through the invention and adoption of slang terms, sometimes through borrowing from other languages. If the dialect-speakers remain separated for a sufficiently long time, each dialect will become a new language, unintelligible to the other.

This process is still evident around us. The differences between British and American English are much greater than many people realize. In the United States, prior to the development of mass radio communication, dialect formation proceeded rapidly in various regions. In our time it is still possible to distinguish a person's regional home through his speech pattern. And there are still dialects which can be ascribed to social class origins rather than regional origins, such as the language spoken in the city ghetto.

### Language Symbolism

There is no such thing as a primitive language. One language may contain fewer nouns than another language, because there are fewer items in the cultural inventory of the people involved. But every language is capable of expressing the cultural needs of a particular people. It may do so in different fashions; it may have different tense forms or grammatical rules, but it is still a highly symbolic, infinite, and arbitrary system of symbols that enables people of a given society to communicate not only direct messages, but also shared philosophies, ideologies, images.

A language is symbolic in nature. Words are regarded in many societies as having inherent power themselves. Among some people, an individual's name is known only to his kin. He is addressed by a nickname, since knowing his name is regarded as equivalent to having power over him. This is similar to the concept by which many people avoid mentioning their deity by name, this being regarded as a dangerous misuse of power. The French have been particularly conscious of the power of symbolism in language. In 1972 they convened a meeting of scholars to erase from the French language such Americanisms as *le weekend,* and *le drugstore,* which, among other words, indicate the extensive contact between the United States and France. The French regard such words as symbolic of a growing Americanization of the French people, particularly young, urban people.

Symbolism in language is both a boon and a danger. Without it we could not enjoy poetry, nor the imagery of good prose, nor, indeed, the ideas of great philosophers. But the inherent danger is that symbolic use of words can also delude people. The most obvious example of this is advertising, which uses language to suggest that the use of a particular product will make ordinary people glamorous and alluring. Or we are told that certain products are "better." Better than what? Better than another product? Or better than the product was last year? Or better than nothing?

There are even more subtle symbols in language. In the United States, for example, the War Department changed to the Defense Department. MacDill Air Force Base was, until 1972, the home of Strike Command. It is now the home of Readiness Command. We have not disarmed; we have changed our phrasing. The verbiage in a political campaign, not to mention a session of Congress, is sufficient to convince one that language can be used to obfuscate as well as to communicate.

Language is a tool, but it can be turned into a weapon. One must be alert to the possibility of being deluded by the use of language. We call it being "conned," and we generally associate it with commercial transactions. We must be equally aware of the potential for being conned politically and personally. How often, in personal transactions, do we use the phrase, "We must get together sometime!" to avoid a more binding commitment to a definite appointment? And have you ever tried to really answer "How are you?" Language is a symbolic system. It may be used for illumination or delusion, just as all symbols may be used. Certain words, innocuous in themselves, conjure up angels or demons for us emotionally. "Red" may represent a deadly enemy.

## Written Language

So far we have been discussing the use of language primarily as a spoken medium of communication, involving the use of symbols. The introduction of writing was a phenomenal step in the evolution of communication. We now believe that written systems came into being about 3200 B.C. in the Middle East. Written language has great advantages over oral language in terms of communication. Obviously, the written record is more durable than spoken communication. Writing can be read long after the writer has left the scene. Writing can be transmitted over distances that cannot be covered by the human voice. Writing can be more accurate than speech (though often it is not). Although a spoken narrative tends to become more distorted with increasing numbers of retellings, written language, too, can often be distorted. There are dead kings in Egypt and Mesopotamia who would have had to have been superhuman to have accomplished all that their monuments claim. In our time, too, written messages can be misleading. Too often, people feel that anything in print is factual, when it may merely be another form of symbolic deception.

Sometimes the written word is regarded as having magical properties in and of itself. Some people wear or use scraps of paper containing certain phrases from the Koran, the Bible, or other sacred texts as amulets to ward off evil or apply them to various parts of the body to cure disease.

Writing seems to have developed through several stages. The earliest writing was in the form of *pictographs*. Each character was a drawing of an object, and when read one after the other, a sentence was made. The earliest Chinese character meaning "man" is a rough stick-figure. Through time, the need for speed and accurate reproduction led to the development of more symbolic notations. Eventually, the pictorial form of writing gave way to a more abstract, flexible alphabet, whereby sounds could be combined to give meaning.

Our alphabet was invented in the Middle East, perhaps by the Phoenicians, some time around 3000 B.C. The medium for notation differed from area to area. The Sumerians, for example, marked on clay tablets with a stylus. The Egyptians used reeds, which they pressed and dried, then painted upon. The reed and the resulting writing paper are called *papyrus*. It is from this that we get the word *paper*. In the New World are carvings in rocks, some of which have been deciphered as calendrical symbols. Others have not as yet been deciphered. Translation is difficult because we do not know whether the writing is alphabetical or not, whether it should be read left to right or up and down. Deciphering a new language is difficult even with modern computer techniques. Jean Champollion deciphered ancient Egyptian by using the Rosetta Stone, which was inscribed with a statement written in ancient Egyptian hieroglyphics, the same statement in cursive Egyptian, and, finally, the same statement in Greek. He was thus able to translate the hieroglyphics from knowing Greek.

### Anthropology and Linguistics

Anthropologists are interested in the study of language for both theoretical and practical purposes. Anthropologists study language *diachronically* and *synchronically*. The diachronic study of language means the study of how language changes through time. This kind of information tells us a great deal about the origins of different groups of people and, as we have seen, about their relationships with other groups. The synchronic study of language, however, is of most interest to anthropologists. Synchronic linguistics means the study of language as it is at the present time.

Linguistic anthropologists are concerned with the symbolic use of language. They analyze the terms used to address kin, and they deduce the types of relationships that exist. They also analyze the way verb tenses are used and the myriad ways a society expresses its world view through the use of language.

For the anthropoloist who does not have the special training of the linguist, however, the study of synchronic linguistics is still most important. Anthropologists contact people whose language is little known to the outside world. We tend to think of languages in terms of Indo-European or Oriental tongues, without realizing there were many native Indian languages, for example, spoken on the North American continent. One of the first tasks of the anthropologist was to compile dictionaries and grammars of these hitherto unknown languages when he encountered them.

But there is a deeper and more important reason for the field anthropologist to learn the language of the people with whom he is working. When he goes to study a particular culture, he must establish a good working relationship with the people he wishes to study. Unfortunately, the anthropologist is seldom the first member of Western civilization to contact people. Others have been there before—soldiers, administrators, health teams—all, with good intent, attempting to change the ways of the people. Attempts are made to change their methods of raising food, attempts are made to move them, attempts are made to cure their ills, and even to change their belief systems. No people can accept with equanimity the idea that everything they have been doing for thousands of years is wrong, and so they are likely to distrust on sight any representative of Western culture. The anthropologist thus has the task of establishing a relationship of trust so that he can do his work. Many have found that the best way to convince people that you really want to learn about them instead of change them is to do so by learning their language rather than teaching them your language. It is wonderful to watch the patience of people who painfully instruct a novice in the language. It is a measure of their relationship when people laugh at the misuse and abuse of the language by the anthropologist, as they would with a child. Out of these efforts grows not only the ability to communicate in words, but also a communication of the purposes of the anthropologist, the one person who enters this strange world not to change it, not to belittle it, but to understand it.

# CHAPTER 7

# Why Dig Holes in the Ground?

Among the four branches of anthropology, archaeology seems most often to capture the fancy of the public. There is something a bit like a good detective story, something adventurous and rewarding about digging into man's past.

But the professional archaeologist is more than just a digger of holes; he is also an anthropologist. He digs up the past not just for exotic objects, but for the same reasons that the anthropologist works with living cultures: he wants to find out how the people lived, how they got their food, and how they spent their time. It is important that he know all these things because an archaeological site is a culture that no longer exists. Why does it no longer exist? Did it grow into something else, and, if it did, what steps did it take? Or did it die? If so, why?

Archaeology is the branch of anthropology that adds the dimension of time to the study of culture. It helps us understand the process of cultural change. By what stages did man's social organization change from small bands of hunters to great civilizations? Why do great old civilizations no longer exist? Is there a regular process of becoming civilized? Are there dangers inherent in civilizations that cause them to decline and "fall?" To know the answers to these questions is to know what we were, what we are, and what we may become.

To the professional archaeologist, a broken shard of pot or a fossilized bit of corn is often more revealing than the finest museum piece. Long before we had professional archaeology, we had gifted and dedicated amateurs. Fortunately, we still have reputable amateurs, usually members of amateur archaeological societies who work closely with professionals. But we also have "pot-hunters" whose intent is not to gain knowledge from the site of an ancient city but to loot the site of saleable objects. There are stringent laws in almost all states of the United States and in almost all foreign nations that provide for returning the loot of pot-hunters to the country of origin. Moreover, the pot-hunters themselves are subject to harsh sentences if apprehended, because, in looting a site, pot-hunters destroy all access to the kinds of information archaeologists are after. Once destroyed, a site cannot usually be reconstructed. Once looted, a site is destroyed. And so, the professional archaeologist battles not only the erosion of time but also the greed of fellow humans.

### Techniques of the Archaeologist

Despite these difficulties, it is truly remarkable how much knowledge archaeologists have gained about man's past. We know much more now than we did just ten or twenty years ago. What has been learned has given anthropologists new insights into the nature of man and his cultures. There are now techniques available for more accurate dating of sites and for more accurate analysis of animal and plant remains. Chemistry, physics, geology, botany, biology, and a host of relatively new sciences— paleobotany, paleozoology—have tremendously expanded our abilities to analyze a site.

Among the most spectacular discoveries in this field is the dating of organic specimens by measuring the amount of radioactive carbon ($C^{14}$) in a given specimen. Before the discovery of this technique, specimens were dated by correlating them with the geological strata in which they were found, or with similar specimens whose placement in sequences was known. This is known as *relative dating*. The term *absolute dating* has been used to describe dates achieved through radiocarbon testing and related methods. However, this is misleading, because such dates necessarily have a margin for error which may be 250 years or more. It would be more accurate to describe this method as a form of time placement.

Briefly, Libby proved that radioactive carbon exists in a constant ratio in the atmosphere. Through photosynthesis, all living vegetation absorbs carbon 14 in a constant proportion. Animals, of course, eat plants and thus also absorb radioactive carbon. Upon the death of an organism, it ceases to absorb carbon, and the radiocarbon content starts to decay into nitrogen

($N^{14}$). The rate of this decay is indicated by the half-life of $C^{14}$, which is now calculated at 5,730 years, plus or minus 40 years. The *half-life* is the time needed for half of a given amount of a substance to decay. So by determining the amount of $C^{14}$ and $N^{14}$ in a given specimen, an approximate date can be given for the specimen's age.

The amount of radioactive carbon in the atmosphere depends upon cosmic ray activity, which differs from time to time. It is likely that man's recent nuclear bomb activities have altered the amount of $C^{14}$ in the atmosphere, hence in living samples. Moreover, there is the principle of *indeterminacy,* as given in Chapter 1, involved with any given sample. For these and other reasons, radiocarbon dates should only be accepted with a margin for error.

## Artifacts

There are some factors science cannot change. One of these is the factor of *differential survival*. Some materials rot faster than others and are therefore almost never preserved. When we are dealing with the culture of the Australopithecines, if we can speak of their "culture" at all, we are talking about millions of years. It has been speculated that the Australopithecines used tools of bone, teeth, and antler horn. Some objects made of these materials survive from this period and may be so interpreted. However, if the Australopithecines wove grasses or carved wooden objects, we will never know about it, short of some fortuitous marvel of preservation. For this reason, archaeologists tend to associate early man with stone tools. There is some feeling, probably justified, that archaeologists tend to stress hunting as a subsistence activity beyond its actual importance to the diet of early man, because vegetable material does not survive, while stone hunting implements do.

The most characteristic type of tool associated with Australopithecines is a simple rough tool, a hammerstone (see Figure 6). It is simply a cobble, which may have been picked up and used as-is, or with a minimum of chipping. Certainly it was in no way a finely worked product.

It has been suggested (Bordes 1968:37–38) that the Australopithecines hunted baboons using thigh bones as weapons. They seem to have used caves as a habitation and to have brought select portions of game home with them. Beyond this, very little is known about the culture of the Australopithecines. We can

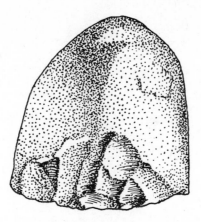

FIGURE 6. **Pebble tool or hammerstone, the earliest tool; associated with Australopithecus. (After a photograph courtesy of the American Museum of Natural History.)**

really talk with some authority only about the period associated with Homo erectus, some 800,000 years ago.

### Remains of Homo Erectus

Homo erectus had already spread into Europe and Asia, and we find evidence of cultural differentiation there. This was no doubt representative of adaptations to differing environments. In Europe and Africa, Homo erectus made a tool we call a *hand axe* (see Figure 7). It is a core tool, a nodule of flint roughly pear-shaped, chipped along both sides, and tapered to a point. It served as an all-purpose tool—one could gouge with it, cut with it, and hammer with it. It persisted with small modifications for 400,000 to 500,000 years.

In Asia, the tool of choice was something we call a *chopper-chopping tool*. It, too, was made of flint but was shaped with a sharpened, rounded edge at one side, and a flat, unsharpened edge at the other.

Fortunately, a cave site in China yielded more information about the life of Homo erectus, at least life as lived in a cave in China. The most dramatic thing to be said about Homo erectus is that he made a significant step in the humanizing process: he learned to use fire. Since fire-making is a difficult skill, and we find no direct evidence of tools for that purpose, we cannot state with certainty that he made fire, but we can tell that he used it, for there are hearths in the cave. Can you imagine what a tre-

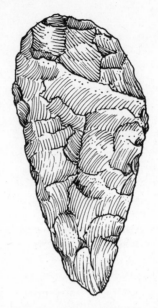

FIGURE 7. **Hand axe or biface, a tool that was distributed from East Africa to North Africa and Europe. (After a photograph courtesy of the American Museum of Natural History.)**

mendous invention that was? In the first place, fire gave light and heat, making the cave more habitable. Second, it could be used to frighten off animals. And third, but by no means the least important factor, fire enabled Homo erectus to cook his food. This enabled him to feed infants, invalids, and aged persons who could not chew raw meat. It also probably also enabled him to make better weapons of fire-hardened wood.

Fire represented the first major innovation on the road to civilization. When we think of the significance of fire, it would be well to bear in mind that nearly every invention of our time is based on the use of fire. One can imagine how a fire was tended and preserved, which must have been a major responsibility. We find echoes of that first fire-tending through time. Most places of worship have an eternal flame. Heroes' graves are decorated with eternal flames. In Rome, seven vestal virgins were employed to guard the sacred fire. And in the ancient civilizations of the New World, calendrical cycles were marked by the extinguishing of all fires, fasting, prayer, ritual, and then cleansing of the body, donning finery, and feasting to celebrate the rekindling of the sacred fire. Culture is cumulative, and the awe man probably felt at his first conquest of nature remains with us in symbolic form.

Homo erectus had other characteristics we may not admire so much. He seems to have been a cannibal, cracking the bones of the dead for marrow. But a curious practice seems to have been followed. The hole at the base of some skulls seems to have been enlarged and the brain removed. This seems to have been done only to certain skulls. Did Homo erectus have a taste for cooked brain? Or was he already pointing the way to some form of ritual cannibalism? Perhaps he recognized the brain as the seat of individuality and ate the brains of selected revered ancestors or honored enemies. We know that until recently this was the practice in New Guinea and in parts of the Amazon basin where eating the brain of honored dead was a way of trying to attain admired characteristics.

For hundreds of thousands of years, man survived and prospered. His population increased. He spread throughout Europe, Asia, and Africa. His cultural advances, slow though they were, enabled him to survive glaciations, to enter and live in new territories. And all the time, his physical form was modifying by processes of natural selection.

### Remains of Neanderthal Man

When we reach the period of about 100,000 years ago, we recognize that man has entered a new stage. This is the era of *Homo sapiens neandertalensis*, or Neanderthal Man. This, remember, is the creature portrayed by modern cartoonists—the cave-man, brutish, cruel.

Let us now look at the picture revealed by modern excavation techniques. Solecki, who has been excavating in Shanidar Cave in Iraq for more than a decade, tells us a great deal about the life of Neanderthal Man (Solecki 1971). Yes, he was a hunter, but he seems to have been neither brutish nor cruel. Shanidar Cave was inhabited by Neanderthals for 60,000 years. There are evidences of a considerable variability in the population, some showing characteristics we associate with a "classic" type, others that bear more resemblance to modern man.

Neanderthal Man made his tools out of flint, but he used a new technique. Instead of using a whole core of flint as an all-purpose tool, he shaped the core, and by some fine knowledge of techniques, he knocked flakes off the core and then shaped the flakes to serve his needs. He made scrapers (see Figure 8), and heart-shaped flakes which may have been spear points.

He lived in groups that included people of both sexes and all

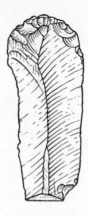

FIGURE 8. Neanderthal scraper. This is the most typical Neanderthal tool made from a flake and was probably used to scrape skins to make clothing. (Courtesy American Museum of Natural History.)

ages. In Shanidar Cave, two notable insights into the life of Neanderthal Man are preserved. For one thing, Neanderthal's life at Shanidar was disrupted several times when the cave roof fell in. This preserved the skeletons of people who were in the cave when the roof fell. One of the more interesting skeletons was of an old man who had been sitting at the rear of the cave, near a warming fire. The remains showed that the man had been blind from birth, and he had a withered arm, probably also from birth. Surely, in a hunting culture, particularly one supposedly so brutish, such a useless individual would have been left to die. But he was not. He must have been tended and fed and kept alive until old age when the roof collapsed.

Perhaps more significant from the viewpoint of the anthropologist was that the people at Shanidar, when they could, dug their dead out of the rubble, and re-buried them. Solecki collected soil samples from the graves and submitted them to a paleobotanist, who found that the soil was heavily laden with the pollen of flowers that grew a short distance from Shanidar, all of which bloomed at the same time. Quite simply, the burials were accompanied by floral offerings—hence the name of Solecki's book, *Shanidar: The First Flower People.* This discovery indicates that in addition to living in groups, Neanderthal had an ideology or a custom that he could communicate to his fellows. Why did he bury his dead? Other Neanderthal graves have shown us that human remains were usually rubbed with red ochre, a red-colored mineral. Did Neanderthal recognize that the difference between sleep and death was visible in skin coloration? Did he try to revive the dead? Did he bury them to keep their bodies from being eaten by animals, or did he have a concept of a hereafter? We do not know, but whatever he believed, he was able to communicate. He shared a cultural tradition with his fellows. He was fully human—and humane as well.

### Remains of Modern Man

Through time the classic Neanderthal type gave way to the type more closely resembling modern man. Dates are approximate, but most anthropologists agree that modern man existed by 40,000 years ago. As one would expect, the tool-making techniques had been greatly refined. Instead of one all-purpose tool, man now had a tool kit, still made of flint, but made by the prepared-core technique. This permitted a more economical use of flint since a single core could produce many specialized tools. We now find awls, knives, and arrowheads, which we call *points*. Some of the fine points are delicate works of art and mark the high point in man's development as a hunter (see Figures 9 and 10). In western Europe, particularly northern Spain and southern France, it would seem that game was plentiful.

This region is best known for the existence of cave art. Far back in the dark recesses of caves, using stone lamps filled with animal fat, with pigments of mineral and vegetable origin, and with brushes made of twigs, man covered cave walls with amaz-

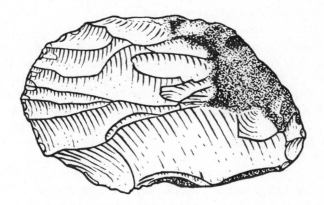

FIGURE 9.    **Homo sapiens' flint blade tool, from a Neanderthal tool kit. (Courtesy American Museum of Natural History.)**

FIGURE 10. Solutrean laurel leaf, an extremely fragile blade which was probably more ceremonial than utilitarian.

ingly beautiful and realistic pictures of animals. We recognize horses, bulls, deer. There are relatively few drawings of men, although some do exist. Paintings are superimposed upon older paintings, and the walls seem to vibrate to the rhythms of animal hooves. Why? What did these paintings mean to early man? The most obvious answer, and that given by early investigators, was that man practiced a kind of hunting magic; he "captured" the animals in paint that he might really capture them in the field. Later, during the epidemic of Freudian theories that swept the scientific world, it was postulated that certain animals were symbolic of one sex, whereas other animals symbolized the opposite sex. What significance this had to early man was never explained, but it was presumed he had problems similar to our own. In 1972, Alexander Marshack proposed the most acceptable interpretation thus far. But before we examine that interpretation, we must look at some other aspect of the art of this period.

In addition to the cave art, there is a great deal of portable art—objects of bone and ivory, some baton-shaped, which have animals carved upon them. These objects are usually bordered with incisions. Other pieces of portable art have been called "venuses," because they are stylized sculptures of females, with strong emphasis on their sexual characteristics and little delineation of facial features or limbs.

Marshack started his studies by examining the portable objects of bone and ivory. By studying the incisions under a microscope, he found they could not have been merely a decorative design. Rather, the incisions seem to have been made at different times using different tools. Marshack suggests that man was "time-factoring" (Marshack 1972), meaning that man was aware of the lunar cycle and that he was counting off periods of the moon. Whether or not it was the lunar cycle that was being counted, the ability of man to count anything had not been suspected for this early period. Marshack also studied the images on these objects and found that not only were recognizable animals portrayed, but so were fish. Was there some correlation between marking off periods of time and the type of game or fish available?

From this point, Marshack goes into the study of the cave art. He points out that along with the pictures of pregnant mares are what appear to be depictions of grasses. Along with bulls are other types of plants. Marshack suggests that cave art was nothing less than a calendar of game types associated with seasons marked by stages in the development of plants. Hunting man kept his own calendar. We have long known that the earliest civilizations were marked by their interest in astronomy, but we have never suspected that the origins of this interest occurred so far back in time. And yet, what is more logical than that man who lived by hunting and by gathering wild plants should be acutely aware of the change of seasons and seek to remember in what order game and plants are available?

As to the venus-figures Marshack points out that, although some were carefully carved and some were carved into rock walls, others seem only sketchily made. Marshack suggests that the more deliberately carved figures were associated with shrines dedicated to childbearing. The more haphazard carvings may have been carved at the time of a particularly difficult delivery, for that case alone, later to be discarded. We know that even today, in simple societies, childbirth constitutes a real risk for both mother and child. It is entirely reasonable to suppose that early man, or woman, took measures to minimize the danger.

## After the Pleistocene

The long period of time stretching from the Australopithecines through the development of modern man and up until about 15,000 years ago in Europe and the Near East is called the *Paleolithic period* ("Old Stone Age"). Australopithecus and Homo erectus belong to the segment of time we call the Lower Paleolithic. Neanderthal is consigned to the Middle Paleolithic, and modern man from about 40,000 to 15,000 years ago lived in the Upper Paleolithic. This period is called the *Pleistocene,* the time of glaciers.

At the end of the Pleistocene, the glaciers receded. The climate in Europe changed. Large game animals, which lived primarily on moss and lichens that grow at the foot of glaciers, receded with the glaciers. The cool steppe climate gave way to warmer forests. Areas which earlier were warm became hot and arid. Most important, the melting of the glaciers caused the sea level to rise; streams became rivers, marshes became lakes.

A new adaptation had to be made by man, as his environment changed drastically. This is the period designated as the *Post-Pleistocene* (Binford and Binford 1968:313). It must be understood that the recession of the glaciers was a gradual affair. The Post-Pleistocene period involved different changes in various environments at various times. One cannot stipulate a specific time for the worldwide changes involved in Post-Pleistocene adaptations. One can merely say that man's adaptations, through inventions and the spread of ideas and techniques, manifested themselves in different parts of the world at different times and resulted in radically altered subsistence strategies. Traditionally, archaeologists have divided the Post-Pleistocene in Europe and Asia into an early period, the *Mesolithic,* and a later period, the *Neolithic* ("New Stone Age").

In Europe, the Mesolithic is marked by certain distinctive changes. Great cave art ceased to be practiced. Instead of finely carved animals on bone and ivory, we have painted pebbles. The early archaeologists, measuring man's development in terms of artistic expression, thought that the Mesolithic marked a period of decline—the "fall" of the great hunting cultures. We know today that it marked, instead, a period of intensive innovation, of adaptation to new conditions, and it was a necessary prelude to the evolution of higher social organizations.

The tool that marks the Mesolithic is the *microlith,* a flint tool about one-half inch long shaped in a triangle, lunate, or circle. Useless by themselves, microliths must be affixed to deer antlers in order to be functional. When you implant a number of the triangular microliths into the inner curve of a deer antler, you get a primitive scythe (see Figure 11). In this crucial period, then, man was intensifying his dependence on plant foods, thus laying the foundation for his later domestication of plants and animals.

It was at this time, too, that man showed his continuing ability to overcome the environment through cultural innovation. From Star Carr, a cave in England, comes the first evidence of an oar. Man, faced with rivers and lakes, developed means of water transport. At this time man first domesticated an animal, the dog. We should pause here to distinguish between domestication and taming. *Domestication* means that man interferes with the breeding process of a species of plant or animal to produce a particular type. *Taming*, on the other hand, is reducing a particular animal from its native wild state. The dog may have been man's companion in hunting for a long time; however, it was not until the Mesolithic that man started to breed dogs for special purposes.

FIGURE 11. Microliths mounted in wood, bone, or antler. These were the earliest composite tools. Stone pieces are fixed into the handle with resin.

It may also be presumed that at this time man became aware of the special properties of certain plants, such as cereal grasses. The scythe described above is evidence that man found a way to cut such grasses in quantity. He may also have started to tame goats and sheep. All this was necessary groundwork for the next major stage in man's cultural evolution, the Neolithic, the later Post-Pleistocene form of adaptation.

During the Neolithic, man ceased to depend on flint as the only medium for tools. He began to use harder stones and to grind them to suit his needs. However, to the anthropologist, this aspect of the Neolithic is of little importance.

Gordon Childe, the great British archaeologist, referred to the Neolithic as a "revolution." Although we are now aware of the fact that the long period of the Mesolithic was preparatory for the Neolithic, we can no longer regard the Neolithic as revolutionary in terms of suddenness, we do regard it as revolutionary in impact.

The primary innovation of the Neolithic was the domestication of plants and animals. For the first time in his millions of years of history, man no longer had to follow game and grasses. He domesticated them and was able to count on a fairly regular supply of food. According to Flannery (1965), domestication of plants and animals involved "a long process of changing ecological relationships between groups of men (living at varying altitudes and in different environmental settings) and the locally available plants and animals which they had been exploiting on a shifting seasonal basis."

Not only did man selectively breed both plants and animals for useful characteristics, but he also transported them to new environments and encouraged mutations that enabled them to thrive there. The sparse, simple hunting bands gave way to settled villages, with concomitant need for social control. Land, which prior to this time was just terrain hunted over, became a valuable property, to be defended and maintained.

The Neolithic stage appeared at different times in different areas of the world. Evidence from Thailand indicates that plants and animals were domesticated there sometime between 20,000 and 8,000 years before the present (Solheim 1972). If the earlier date is chosen, the Neolithic may have begun in Southeast Asia fully 5,000 years prior to its inception in the Middle East. The dates we usually accept for Middle Eastern domestication are around 10,000 years ago. But in the western hemisphere, domestication did not take place until about 8,000 years before the present. When we speak of the Neolithic, it is better to think of it as an evolutionary stage, rather than a specific time period.

Archaeologists have shown that every continent and every race contributed to the variety of animals and plants that were domesticated. Corn and potatoes were the prime plants cultivated in the western hemisphere. Wheat, oats, barley, sheep, and goats come to us from the Middle East. Horses and pigs seem to have derived from Europe, and chickens and rice from the Orient. Millet and ground-nuts are suggested domesticants for Africa. It should not be supposed that plants or animals were domesticated only once in a single place. For example, strong evidence suggests that corn was independently domesticated in both Mexico and Peru at about the same time (MacNeish 1970). Both plants and animals were probably domesticated at about the same time. Large stands of semi-wild grasses would naturally attract grazing animals. Man, seeking food, would be brought into contact with both, and through the process of learning the habits of the animals and taming them, and learning the nature of plant reproduction, he would eventually domesticate both.

Some of these processes of domestication have left their mark on present day society. The bull-fight, for example, is not a sport but a ritual commemorating man's mastery of the bull. When we recall that the first domesticated cattle were huge beasts, capable of killing a man easily, the struggle between man and bull must indeed have been epic.

Another reminder of more ancient customs is the prohibition by both Jews and Moslems against eating pork. It was recently suggested that the pig, which usually thrives on acorns in a forested area, would be a non-economic domesticant in the Middle East (Harris 1972). It gives no milk or eggs; it would not thrive on desert or oasis foliage, so it would have to be fed from the meager store man had reserved for himself in that arid area. The pig cannot even be used to pull things, as can the horse or the ox. In fact, it would be a luxury that the Middle East could ill afford, and the religious proscriptions against eating pork may have been an attempt to discourage its breeding in that area. Another suggestion is that the pig was an unsuitable domesticant in an area where herding and pastoral nomadism were prevalent (Flannery 1965). Although the pig was domesticated by 6,000 B.C. in the Zagros Mountain valleys of the Mesopotamian area, its use in Mesopotamia never became widespread.

In addition to the domestication of plants and animals, the Neolithic is marked by two more outstanding contributions. It was during this period that the wheel was invented and pottery came into use.

The wheel, like the domestication of fire, was a primary invention in that so many later inventions are founded upon it. We do not know for sure just where this early invention took place, and, again, it might have been reached independently by several cultures.

Pottery is of prime importance to the archaeologist, because the style, shape, and decoration of potshards are often his most substantive clue to the identity of the culture. Ceramic styles are individual and, like fingerprints, identifiable. But, the existence of pottery is indicative of something even more important. Pottery is only of use to a settled society. We know from the observation of nomadic societies today that, although they have access to pottery, they prefer to use leather bags or baskets, which are not so breakable. The existence of pottery in a site indicates to the archaeologist that he is dealing with a people who remain in one location most of the time, a settled people.

The Neolithic, then, is the stage which made possible all the later stages of man's cultures. We still eat the plants and animals domesticated during the Neolithic. The wheel is a major component of today's technology. And pottery is still found in our homes both decoratively and usefully. In the next chapter we discuss the rise of civilization, recognizing that the roots of civilization go back into the time of very early man.

# CHAPTER 8

# Lost Cities
# and Buried Treasure

At least part of the romance of archaeology is due to the discoveries of "lost cities" in jungles, the uncovering of treasures in tombs as fabulous as those of King Tutankhamen. One stands in awe at the impressive site of the ruins of Teotihuacán, the first city in the western hemisphere. We wonder how such ruins came to be. We wonder who the people were who created them. Often, in ignorance or ethnocentrism, we do not credit the ancestors of the present inhabitants with the necessary skill. We search out such unlikely creators as the lost tribes of Israel, the mythical inhabitants of Atlantis or Mu, and, more recently, even creatures from outer space.

These monumental works are hallmarks of that stage of the evolution of social organization called *civilization*. It is incorrect to speak of Navajo civilization, or Eskimo civilization. These peoples have cultures, surely, but these cultures have not evolved into that stage anthropologists designate as civilization. Most anthropologists would agree that civilization can be defined on the basis of seven criteria (Lanning 1967:3): intensive agriculture; large, dense populations; efficient distribution systems; diversity of settlement patterns; state structures; intensive social stratification; and extensive occupational specialization. Only a few places in the world reached this stage independently. Traditionally, we consider Peru-Bolivia, Mesoamerica, Mesopotamia, China, and possibly India to be these areas.

Anthropologists are deeply interested in the rise of civilization. We want to know why so few places in the world reached this stage indigenously. We want to know the process by which it was reached. We want to know if the process was similar in the different environments, given differing histories of societies in the Old World and the New World. (Archaeologists refer to all of Europe, Asia, and Africa as the Old World. North and South America are considered the New World.) Many anthropologists have worked for a long time to answer these questions. As a result, theories have been defined and refined, proposed and revised. Much work remains to be done before these questions can be resolved. Let us examine the rise of civilization in the context of New World archaeology.

## Civilization in the Americas

During the Ice Ages, water was frozen into glaciers, thus lowering the sea level around the world. The Bering Strait, the narrow strip of water which separates Alaska from Siberia, was then a land mass. Some time during the final glacial episode, man crossed that land bridge, probably to hunt animals. Krieger (1964) would date this 35,000 to 40,000 years ago. Other anthropologists think this happened more recently, but a consensus would probably be reached at a figure of 20,000 to 25,000 years ago.

Man spread along ice-free corridors throughout North and South America. There are secure radiocarbon datings of 8700 B.C. associated with projectile points from the tip of South America (Willey 1971:48). These indicate not only the antiquity of man's habitation of the New World, but also the fact that he came here as a hunter and pursued this way of life for a very long time. In some parts, notably the Great Plains, Canada, and southern South America, hunting and gathering remained the primary, if not the only, subsistence strategy until European contact.

Elsewhere, however, recession of the last glaciers caused changes in the environment to which people responded with differing subsistence strategies. It would be profitable at this point to examine the Tehuacán Valley sequence (MacNeish 1967), one of the best archaeological examples of the kind of changes which occurred through time.

The Tehuacán Valley is located in south-central Mexico, in the state of Puebla. The area has a hot, dry climate and is surrounded by mountains. These mountains deflect rainstorms from some areas, causing variable states of aridity within the valley. There are rivers, notably the Rio Santo Domingo and the

Rio Salado. However, these streams and their tributaries are not filled with water throughout the year (MacNeish 1967, Vol. I: p. 35). The dryness of the area helped preserve vegetal remains which added immeasurably to our knowledge of early corn cultivation. The sequence, as established by MacNeish from various sites in Tehuacán Valley is as follows:

*Stage 1:    Ajuereado.* This stage began at some early date not as yet established and persisted until about 6800 B.C. The population consisted of twelve to twenty-eight people, living in small, wandering bands. Wet season and dry season camps were distinguished. They lived by hunting, trapping, and gathering wild plants.

*Stage 2:    El Riego.* Dates are 6800 to 5000 B.C. The population was now four times the original size. The little bands still wandered from wet season camps to dry season camps, but they grouped together annually during the spring to form a large band (macroband). The subsistence emphasis had shifted from hunting to plant collecting. The use of squash and chile is demonstrated.

*Stage 3:    Coxcatlan.* The dates are from 5000 to 3000 B.C. The population increased to ten times the original number. People lived most of the time in semi-sedentary macrobands, separating into microbands to disperse to dry season camps. Chile and squash are known to be domesticated early in this stage. Corn, beans, and gourds became domesticated during this stage. The major subsistence technique was agriculture, with hunting and trapping becoming supplemental to the basic diet.

*Stage 4:    Abejas and Purron.* This stage is dated 3000 to 1500 B.C. The population is estimated to be forty times the original. People lived in semipermanent villages composed of a number of microbands living together and only occasionally went off to hunting camps. These people were full-time agriculturalists who had probably begun to hybridize corn to achieve a better grade of corn. The Purron stage, as distinguished from the Abejas, is marked by the introduction of pottery.

*Stage 5:    Ajalpan and Santa Maria.* The dates are 1500 to 200 B.C. The population is now 1,800 to 3,600 people, about a hundred and fifty times that of the Ajuereado stage. During the Abejas stage, people lived in small villages. They grew corn, beans, squash, gourds, chile, and a seed-plant called amaranth. The Santa Maria stage is distinguished by the fact that ceremonial centers and pyramids were constructed.

*Stage 6:    Palo Blanco.* Lasting from 200 B.C. to 700 A.D., the population is estimated at this stage to be 24,000, or a thousand times the original number. People live in permanent villages, only going off to hunting camps in small parties. These villages are built around ceremonial centers. Irrigation agriculture was in full use and resulted in a more balanced diet, as evidenced by fecal analysis. Aqueducts, irrigation ditches, and dams are evident.

*Stage 7: Venta Salada.* During this stage, between 700 and 1500, 120,000 people lived in the area. They were full-time intensive agriculturalists. People lived in various types of communities ranging from cities through towns to small villages. Commerce in salt was also developed. We are now dealing with a stage which unquestionably represents civilization, broadly comparable to civilization in the Old World although differing in such matters as the use of metals, draft animals, and plows.

### Agriculture

This sequence shows a progressive increase in population and a steady increase in dependence upon cultivated food. Attempts to maximize agricultural productivity began as early as the Abejas stage, with its efforts at corn hybridization, and culminated in the Palo Blanco stage, with irrigation, dams, and aqueducts. Going back to the criteria for civilization, we note that intensive agriculture is the first criterion upon which all the other criteria depend.

In some areas where arable land is limited, increasing population pressures have been met by technological efforts to maximize agriculture (Boserup 1965). This is done through such devices as irrigation, making more land available on mountain slopes by building terraces, and the particular Mesoamerican device, the *chinampa*. The chinampa is an artificial island created by trenching out a canal or river and piling the dirt in the center of the river. When the mound is high enough, trees are planted on it to hold the earth. Such "floating gardens" are still in use and can be seen in Xochimilco, Mexico. The food and flowers grown there are transported and sold in Mexico City. The plow and natural and artificial fertilizers by this time had been developed in the effort to maximize agricultural productivity.

Plant and animal domestication in the New World began in "nuclear sites" (Allan, in Ucko, et al. 1972). With increasing population in these areas, agriculture spread to more marginal areas, in which soil fertility was only maintained by such methods as rotation of sites—that is, allowing some land to lie fallow while other land is in use. In other areas, irrigation ditches or other devices made their appearance. These techniques represented attempts on the part of man to gain mastery of the environment. "Mastery of these environments called for concerted action. This required the establishment of coordinating authorities controlling large populations and powerful enough to draft mass labour for the construction of irrigation and other public works. It also involved development planning on a large scale. The controlling authorities, kings, royal officers, nobles and priesthoods, also controlled the surplus of production; they accumulated wealth and power, so long as the surplus continued to increase" (Allan, in Ucko, et al. 1972:223).

On the other hand, others propose that the specialization of crops, caused either by the use of marginal land or by ecological considerations, led to the development of trade networks among agricultural centers. Organized trade networks led to the development of authorities and administrators, who used the surplus to accumulate wealth and power. These ideas are not mutually exclusive. Both systems may have coexisted in the same society, whereas other agricultural societies may have found still other methods to intensify agriculture to maximize food production.

Basic to the rise of civilization, most anthropologists agree, is the intensification of agriculture to the point where a surplus can be stored. Cereal agriculture lends itself well to this criterion, because although a surplus of perishable foodstuffs may regularly occur, mechanisms must be found to consume it before it is spoiled. Cereal grains can be stored against a poor harvest in following years. They can also be collected and redistributed through taxes and tithes. Grain can be measured, and accurate amounts of grain can become a standard of value, as in Mesopotamia and ancient Egypt. Since population tends to grow to the limit of resources, a large and dense population follows the intensification of agriculture. Density is the result of the creation of special areas where administrators function, and to which people are attracted by various needs. Intensification of agriculture results in specialization in one or a small number of crops which must be distributed over networks in exchange for other materials that may be lacking. Internally, intensification makes it possible for some individuals to be freed from agricultural pursuits to follow other occupations. Yet they must be fed, so efficient distribution systems must operate within the civilization and between the civilized society and other societies. Diversity of settlement patterns comes about because some people remain in villages, raising the crops, while towns arise out of the need for intermediary sites for exchange of commodities, and the administrators reside in special places which may be either ceremonial centers or cities, depending on the nature of the ruling elite.

This elite must have the authority to implement the maximization of agriculture. In order to do that, state structures must be institutionalized. The managerial class must have the right to command the obedience of the population above and beyond the loyalties an individual owes to his kinship group. Managers must be able to obtain labor for such massive projects as irrigation works. They must also be able to defend the now permanently valuable land from outsiders who may wish to appropriate it. They need to coerce a surplus of the crop from the producers in order to support their own activities. All this is institutionalized by the creation of state structures.

Development of social classes is the result of the preceding factors. The elite managerial class, be they priests or rulers, are set apart by their authority from the rest of society. Eventually, a ranking, based either on distance in relationship to the rulers or on values placed upon differing occupations, emerges. The basis for social stratification is the access to power of occupational groups or hereditary groups. Thus, there may emerge a class society ranking from most powerful to least powerful: ruler, nobility, military, traders, artisans, farmers, slaves. The number of classes and their order in the power structure varies from society to society.

Extensive occupational specialization is made possible by the intensification of agriculture, which frees some people to perform other functions. Such specialization is necessary because, in a civilized society, there are many other functions than farming to be performed.

This is but a broadly drawn outline of the rise of civilization, so broad, indeed, that it may validly be disputed by those who study the rise of a specific civilization. There is much work yet to be done in this area, and research is ongoing. In fact, in the western hemisphere, archaeologists even dispute the status of one society in whether or not it can be classified as a civilization.

## Mesoamerican Civilization

About 2000 to 1500 B.C., in the swampy isthmus of Tehuantepec, a neck of land that connects highland Mexico with the Yucatán and Central America, some quite remarkable projects were taking place. Archaeologists have discovered a ceremonial center built on the island of La Venta. Not only did this center contain platforms, a pyramid, and several mounds, but, in an area where there is no natural stone, more than a dozen great stone monuments have been found. These range from flat-topped monuments, which have been called altars, to ornately carved upright stones, called *stelae*. As excavations continued, remarkable amounts of buried stone were uncovered. The excavators have called these caches buried offerings. Some of the buried offerings were jade celts (a type of axehead), others were figurines, and perhaps the most remarkable was a set of stones laid out to form the face, or mask, of a jaguar (Coe 1968).

Research indicates that the people who built this ceremonial center lived in small farming villages on the mainland. The island itself was the home of a group of priests who commanded the loyalty of the outlying farmers by maximizing the agricultural potential. Through their observation of the stars, they could predict the onset of alternating wet and dry seasons, thus permitting the farmers to plant two crops a year (Heizer 1960). In return for this service, and in order to emphasize their authority, they extracted labor from the populace, in the form of transporting huge amounts of stone, and regularly rebuilt their sanctuary. They also extracted much wealth in the form of jade, which was the Mesoamerican equivalent of gold. The deity worshipped at this center appears to have been a jaguar, or jaguar-man. The jaguar in South America is the symbol of the spirit, or power of the *shaman,* a powerful priest (Furst, in Benson 1968:143–174).

The people who built and maintained this ceremonial center, who have been called the Olmec (their actual name has been lost in antiquity), evidently carried on a lively trade with the plateau area of Mexico and with the Petén region, which is now part of Guatemala. The Olmec needed salt, obsidian, and stone. They probably exported corn from the surplus achieved through the two-crop system. In any event, their particular style of ceramics, their belief system, the style of their ceremonial centers, and their system of notation became the cultural foundation upon which later Mesoamerican civilizations were built.

There is an ongoing argument among scholars as to whether the Olmec can be classified as a civilization. Coe (1968), pointing to the monumental architecture of the ceremonial centers, the diversity of settlement types between farms and ceremonial center, the sophistication of stonework from which he infers a class of stoneworkers as occupational specialists, and the obvious differentiation between the priesthood who inhabited La Venta and the surrounding agriculturalists, calls this America's first civilization. On the other hand, Sanders and Price (1968) state that the networks of trade which involved the exchange of stone for grain could have been regulated through kinship structures, rather than state structures. They regard the Olmec as a chieftainship in that there were only two classes, the priesthood and the populace, rather than the intensive social stratification present in a civilization. Moreover, the absence of true nucleation in the form of cities and towns negates, in their view, the classification of the Olmec as a civilization. This is, perhaps, the same sort of problem we have noted before, in that stages in an evolutionary progression are subject to varying interpretations.

By 200 B.C. the Olmec culture, having left its mark on the other cultures of Mexico, was in decline. However, in the Valley of Mexico, northeast of present-day Mexico City, the beginnings of the first true city in the Americas, Teotihuacán, were stirring. Millon (1964), who has mapped the city, estimates that it covered three square miles. Population figures are harder to derive, but Sanders and Price (1968:149) estimate that 100,000 people lived in the city at its peak.

The city itself consists of ceremonial pyramids and platforms and a *ciudadella*, which has been interpreted as an administrative center or public edifice. Surrounding these are opulent homes of evidently wealthy and privileged people, and outward from this central core are streets, laid out on a grid pattern, where the residences of artisans and other functionaries are found. Still farther out, on the perimeter, are the homes of poorer people, and eventually the outskirts of the city blend into the surrounding rural areas. There is a particular part of the city where archaeologists have found ceramic wares characteristic of cultures outside the Valley of Mexico, indicating formalized trade relationships with those areas.

There is no question that Teotihuacán represents the full bloom of civilization in the New World. The period in which Teotihuacán was preeminent lasted from about 200 B.C. to 700 A.D. This is known as the Classic period. During this time, the ceremonial centers of the Mayan area were built. It is now evident that the impetus for the growth and proliferation of Mayan sites came from Teotihuacán, although the mechanisms for this and the underlying reasons are as yet poorly understood (Sanders and Price 1968). Again, much work remains to be done before we will know the extent and nature of the far-flung Classic relationships.

It was during this Classic period that some of the finest ceramic ware was made. Each area specialized in its own form of pottery, making it possible for archaeologists to identify ceramics with their points of origin. The people of this time used two calendars, one a religious calendar of 260 days, the other a secular calendar of 365 days. Every 52 years, the calendars would coincide, and that day was celebrated by extensive ritual carried on at the ceremonial centers. A form of writing existed, known to us through carvings of glyphs on monuments. Although we can now read the numerical and calendrical glyphs, the rest of the glyph system has not yet been deciphered.

Unfortunately, modern travelers to Mesoamerica were first impressed by the huge ceremonial centers of the Mayan area. This gave rise to the popular notion of Mayan supremacy among the civilizations of the New World. In fact the Mayan development seems to have been stimulated by and dependent upon the civilization of the Valley of Mexico.

Some time after 600 A.D., that great civilization declined. The reasons for this are as yet poorly understood. They may have been internal, such as several poor crop years or increasingly costly demands of the ruling hierarchy. There is no evidence for such external factors as invasion. For whatever reason, within a hundred years of that date, Teotihuacán was no longer a major power, and even the names of the people who built it were forgotten. Similarly, building of great ceremonial centers in the highland and southern lowland Mayan areas ceased, never to be resumed, and in the northern lowlands, the Yucatán, new forces were at work.

The power vacuum in the Valley of Mexico was filled by a people we call the Toltecs, who founded several cities. Archaeologists dispute whether many of these cities were built during the Classic period and were simply overshadowed by Teotihuacán, or whether they arose only after the Classic period. The era of the Toltecs lasted from about 700 to 1100 A.D. They built upon the existing culture in that they retained the use of pyramids and ceremonial centers, the double calendar, and the glyphic writing.

The Toltecs are thought by present-day Mexicans to be the founders of much of Mesoamerican culture, which is inacccurate. It was during Toltec times that the Quetzalcoatl legend is supposed to have arisen. Quetzalcoatl, which is the actual name of a Toltec ruler, is regarded as the culture hero of Mesoamerica. It was he who supposedly taught the people to plant corn and taught them rules of proper behavior. He was a kindly and good ruler. However, he had a brother who represented all that was negative in Mesoamerican culture, being an advocate of human sacrifice, among other things. Legend has it that Quetzalcoatl, the good ruler, was a man of light complexion with a red beard. He abstained from drink and carousing and altogether was a model of propriety. In the legend, the evil brother plotted against Quetzalcoatl, drugging his food and planting a woman in his room while he slept. When Quetzalcoatl woke from his sleep, he was so shamed by what he thought he had done that he left Mexico, sailing off to the east, promising that he would return. When the Spanish explorer Cortez, who was a white man with a red beard, arrived, the Mexicans thought he was the returning god Quetzalcoatl, and hesitated between placating him and fighting him. Alas, it is only a legend.

In fact, the Toltecs extended their rule to the Yucatán where they built such impressive sites as Chichén Itzá and Mayapan. There was constant warfare and rivalry among the cities which composed the Toltec empire. Alliances were made and broken, and warfare was endemic. Throughout this period, areas more remote from the central plateau retained their individuality, although they were all influenced to some extent by the greater Toltec powers. During Classic times, Mexican influences extended into what is now the United States, in the form of irrigation farmers in the American southwest and mining colonies in the Durango and Sonora areas of Mexico. In the Toltec period, the mining colonies were fortified, as represented by the site of La Quemada. Through this contact, people remote from the Mexican heartland were Mexicanized. Nevertheless, the constant warfare debilitated the Toltecs, and some time around 1100 their dynasty declined.

This time the power vacuum was filled by the people who ruled during the Spanish conquest, the Aztecs. Much of what is written about the Aztecs is based on the chronicles of Spanish priests and warriors and must therefore be understood as having a strong ethnocentric bias. The earliest Europeans to see the Aztec city of Tenochtitlán, over which modern Mexico City is built, were greatly impressed by the clean broad avenues, the buildings decorated by beautiful murals. Even the Spanish priests, bent on converting the infidel, had to admire the cleanliness of the people, the chastity of their women, the bravery of their men.

Much has been made of the Aztec practice of human sacrifice. It is true this was done, but only at special calendrical rituals and, even then, no great numbers of victims were sacrificed. It was only when conquest was imminent that the people, fearing their gods had forsaken them, resorted to an orgy of human sacrifice. In fact, the wars of the Aztecs were far more civilized than that of their conquerors. They often surrounded a village and asked that it surrender and pay tribute. If the village refused, it had the right to send forth a champion who would fight a single Aztec hero. The fight decided the fate of the village.

For all their reputation as a heathen people, one can today count the vast numbers of temples in the Aztec area. It is easy to do this because the Christians leveled every one of them and built a church upon the ruins. In addition to churches, the Aztecs had schools for boys and girls, commoners and nobility. These were remarkable in that the schools for the nobility were much more rigorous than those for the commoners. Boys were expected to show not only respect and piety, but also courage and endurance. They were being trained for leadership which was more exacting than the training needed for simple soldiers.

The first sight of Tenochtitlán, the great Aztec city, with its aqueducts, lakes, and great avenues, led the men of Spain to call it the Venice of the New World. But their ethnocentrism and aggression destroyed it.

The rise of civilization in Mesoamerica is similar but, of course, different in detail from the rise of civilization in other parts of the world. Outside the western hemisphere, the existence of domesticable animals, the early use of metals, and the differences of techniques associated with wheat, barley, and rice cultivation as compared to corn cultivation led to vast differences in the nature of the emerging civilizations. In the Peru-Bolivia area, although the course of the rise of civilization was more similar to Mesoamerica than to anything elsewhere, there were some differences, such as earlier use of metals and the existence of llamas and alpacas. The Inca, like the Aztec, were in the process of carving out a highly developed state when they were overcome by European conquest.

In sum, civilization is a particular level of cultural evolution, reached indigenously by only a few cultures, but which is such a successful adaptation that it has spread widely over the globe. Although civilizations differ in their expressions of the criteria of civilization, and though they may have taken differing routes toward that stage, they share a basic feature. That feature is the intensification of grain agriculture, which makes all the other characteristics possible.

# CHAPTER 9

# It's Human Nature

The last chapter cited numerous instances of conquest, warfare and aggression among peoples. In our time the almost constant threat of war has led thoughtful people to question man's extraordinary capacity for self-destruction.

In recent years the public has been exposed to books written by experts in animal behavior, by dramatists, and by other individuals even less qualified to speak for man. The burden of their message has been to reaffirm what passes for folk wisdom: man is a killer because that is "human nature." Merely knowing this absolves man from attempts to control the uncontrollable, for instance, "Guns do not kill people, people do." Obviously there is nothing that can be done about that—it's human nature.

Let us examine, in the light of previous chapters, the nature of human nature. First, we must make a distinction between *warfare*, with its cool planning, long-term operations, and definite goals, and *rage* or *hostility*, the abrupt loss of control that signals violence.

We have seen that man and the other primates descended from a common ancestor, whose behavior we cannot examine because it is extinct. However, it is more rational to seek clues to human nature among our closest relatives than in such distantly related species as birds or fish.

Rage is not a stranger to the primate world. Everyone is familiar with the gorilla's chest-pounding, a frightening threat gesture. Few people realize, however, that if the gorilla's opponent is not frightened by this display of hostility, the gorilla will retreat. Schaller (1964), who has studied the mountain gorilla, notes no occasions on which the threatening gorilla carries out his threat, although his size alone makes him a formidable opponent. Chimpanzees, too, have tantrums which have appropriately been called *display behavior*. The angry chimp will take to the trees, shake branches, hurl sticks and stones, and scream at the top of his lungs. There are no instances of chimpanzees killing each other during these displays.

Certainly man is capable of great rage and frustration. But man is also capable of much tenderness and kindness. To what extent these capacities are employed is directly related to the cultural milieu in which he is reared. Let us not forget that man is the animal subject to the longest enculturation period of all. His reactions to other people are largely conditioned by his culture.

How does a person in a rage behave? The answer to that differs from society to society. In Borneo, for example, it is considered just another event when a person in a rage runs amok. People gather their children into their houses and close their doors while the enraged individual rampages through the village displaying much the same behavior as the enraged chimpanzee. He yells, stomps, hurls things, breaks things. If some unlucky soul gets in his way, he may be rudely pushed away. But after the rage, the individual settles back to everyday quiet behavior. The villagers go about their business as though nothing unusual had occurred. Among the Semai, a Malaysian people, such violence is unheard of. When one Semai angers another, the victim goes into a condition of sadness, depression, and dejection. At this juncture, either the victim or one of his kin will approach the person who caused the problem and demand compensation be paid, or the two antagonists will negotiate a resolution of the problem. Quarrels do occur, of course, but these are verbal and usually consist of minor name-calling and an attempt to enlist public support for one side or the other. Where the quarrel cannot thus be settled, a headman is asked to arbitrate, and his decisions are morally binding. Anger is avoided. Quarrels are infrequent and regarded as bad because "they scare people." If two Semai honestly dislike each other, they avoid each other (Dentan 1968). If we assume the Semai and ourselves are both descended from Dryopithecines, it would seem that violence is not part of our heritage.

### Instinct versus Learning

The entire problem of how much of man's behavior can be regarded as instinctual is one that needs ventilation. Studies of monkeys have shown that such behavior as copulation and infant rearing, heretofore regarded as instinctive, are indeed learned. Certainly toilet training and sleep habits are learned and the ways people do these activities vary from culture to culture. Why do we make the exception of the expression of rage? Most psychologists now agree that we must be taught to express love, and it follows that we are also taught how to express anger. Eisenberg (1972) finds no evidence of an aggressive instinct as an independent motivational force analogous to hunger. There is no periodicity, no changes in the internal parameters which trigger aggression. The "need" for aggression is stimulated externally, and the stimulus is culturally defined. Some men will kill at an indirect reference to their mother. Other men will endure in silence the most dire threats to their persons or loved ones. With strong cultural bias, many anthropologists would accept only two human instincts: suckling and grasping. All else is learned behavior conditioned by our culture.

In our time we are particularly aware of the faceless crime of the street—the mugger, the rapist, the stranger who threatens our lives. The cry for "law and order" is heard in political campaigns. What does this rise in the reported crime rate indicate for our society? For the anthropologist and the sociologist, such wanton violence indicates deep discontent within the culture. In a large and complex society such as ours, whole groups of people are unable to attain, through normal channels, the style of life our politicians and schools promise. Ever larger groups are cut off from legitimate passage to power. More and more individuals find themselves unable to cope with the complexities of our exceedingly complex societies. All these people feel a deep unrest. They are in the society yet not of the society.

## Violence in Society

In some cultures, people like this would spend their time in meditation. In other cultures, they would become deeply depressed. In our culture, this type of alienation is manifest in a traditionally American way: the cult of violence is acted out. The two-fisted hero bashing in other people's heads on his way to righteousness is a folk figure for us. Our sports are often appreciated in direct proportion to their violence. Violence in sport seems to mirror the amount of violence in the society as a whole. "War and combative type sports therefore do not, as often claimed, act as alternative channels for the discharge of accumulable aggressive tensions. Rather than being functional alternatives, war and combative sports activities in a society appear to be components of a broader culture pattern" (Sipes 1973).

Our very language teems with violence, as in "fight for your rights." In most parts of the country, manliness is equated with violence. Seldom is a small boy allowed to grow up without his "manliness" being challenged by the peer group, and the challenge is met by fistfights. Television and movies have lately come under attack for inducing violence in their watchers. Although much of our TV fare is tasteless, it would be unfair to blame this surge of violence on it. The advertisers who sponsor TV programs are interested in giving the audience what it enjoys to attract larger audiences and more prospective customers. In all likelihood it is the audience which creates TV violence, not vice versa.

We justify violence for a "good" cause, then complain about violence when it discomforts us or endangers our lifestyle. But we do not hold violence in disdain as do the Semai. We have the inherent danger of enculturating all people with the cult of violence. This means that violence will not be reserved for a cause we see as just, but will be used wantonly to relieve the anger and frustration of the repressed, and maliciously by groups hoping to achieve some degree of recognition, and criminally by those so inclined.

What can be done about violence? If you have no faith in the perfectability of human beings, no faith in the humanizing process, you will call for more violence to oppose violence. Arm citizens so they may "fight back." Call out more police, build bigger jails, shoot looters. If, on the other hand, you believe man can be encultured to control his anger and hostilities and channel them into less destructive paths, it will be necessary to put forth a conscious effort to educate ourselves and our children away from violence. This certainly can be done. When violence for whatever reason is abhorred, such behavior is not countenanced. It is not idealized; it is not taught; it is discouraged as uncivilized or as unworthy of human beings.

We have, as humans, infinite capacity for tenderness as well as violence. We make pets of otherwise useless animals. Most of us treat old people and small children with a great consideration, although both can be nuisances. If we face up to our responsibility as self-domesticators, and if we work to regain those qualities of humaneness which have long distinguished mankind from other primates, we can unlearn violence, just as we learned it.

Crime in the streets, violence in the home—these are reflections of our growing individualization. Society has become so large and impersonal that individuals no longer feel interdependent. People are no longer friends and neighbors but strangers. And herein lies the greatest danger to our society, for fragmentation can spell our doom. Perhaps it will be necessary to experiment with alternative residential patterns in order to ameliorate this impersonality. Certainly we will have to redress some of the flagrant injustices in our society. Perhaps we will have to tone down some of our aspirations as a great materialistic society until we can spread the goods more widely. Certainly we will have to relearn responsibility for each other. But all of this will take time. Limiting public access to guns might be helpful.

## Warfare

Turning now to a discussion of warfare, we recognize an immediate difference. The crime of violence triggered by hostility is a crime of passion. But in order to conduct a war, passions must be artificially aroused. Thus there are tales of enemy atrocities, parades with banners and marching bands, handsome uniforms for soldiers (which they do not wear in the field), and all the propaganda effort of which modern nations are capable. Surely, if the people were truly hostile and outraged, all this would not be necessary. In addition, wars are not conducted by people in the throes of rage. Wars are planned, moves are studied, alternatives are calculated. Some people devote their entire lives to plotting how to kill the most people most efficiently. Surely these people do not live out their careers in a permanent state of anger.

Earlier thinkers tried to show that warfare was purely an economic matter. People went to war at the behest of munitions manufacturers, so the notion ran, and once production was socialized, wars would cease. Although anthropologists would agree that much of modern warfare has an economic component, the proposition as a whole is too simplistic for casual acceptance.

Let us examine warfare as it appears in simpler societies, so that we may determine the roots of the modern version.

Vayda (1960) makes a distinction between a raid and warfare. A *raid* is a short-term act of aggression, requiring little or no logistic support. *Warfare*, on the other hand, is the mobilization of a population and all its institutions toward a long-term aggressive or defensive action. Since simpler societies have smaller and fewer institutions, and usually a smaller or poorer economic base, their aggressive activity is confined to raiding. But this raiding may be so frequent as to amount to a perpetual state of siege. The

Dani, who live in Highland New Guinea, are an example of this situation.

Heider (1970:106) reports seventeen instances of battles or raids between the Dugum Dani and their neighbors in a few months' time. Fine rules have been set up. There is a battlefield where the warriors go, dressed in their finery on every day it does not rain. They fling spears at each other, seldom inflicting more than minor wounds. When anyone is wounded, the battle ceases. However, the real object of the "game" is to kill a member of the opposing community. In order to do this, stealth is usually used, and even women and children are considered worthy victims. Dani men keep watch from towers all day to prevent the enemy from infiltrating their land and killing someone. Sometimes the surveillance fails, and someone is killed. The victim's group is notified across the battleground. Time out is taken for the appropriate mourning activities on one side and for victory celebrations on the other. The victim's body is reclaimed by his kin, who for this purpose can cross into enemy territory unchallenged. Then the raiding resumes, with the "loser" now seeking revenge and the equalization of scores by killing the enemy.

The Dani explain the ritual of warfare in terms of their belief in ghosts (Heider 1970:130). The ghosts of their own dead are constantly present and are a threat to the health and economic life of the people. These ghosts can only be placated by the killing of an enemy. Since the enemy shares the same belief system, killing of a member of one group leads to the revenge killing of a member of the other group in an endless feedback system. Heider himself did not find the Dugum Dani to be a particularly aggressive people; rather, he finds warfare a deeply embedded factor in the culture. Warfare is an important factor in proving manhood; it is also a cohesive factor among groups of men. The Dani do not fight for possession of land. Their warfare seems to be an attempt to stabilize existing boundaries. Dying and killing are one of the ways population and land tenure can be stabilized. The belief system rationalizes this behavior.

When we examine the behavior of smaller and simpler societies which hunt and gather plant materials for food, we seldom find any behavior that approaches this kind of thing. They quarrel and sometimes kill, but this is the type of rage behavior against which the society has structured patterns of sanctions and atonements. They do not seem obsessed with territory or the protection of privilege. In hunting and gathering societies, the land over which they hunt is not a permanent possession. Its only importance is the game hunted upon it. Since the technology of these bands is often very weak, animals which may have been speared or shot with a poisoned arrow often live on for days and wander into adjoining territories before they die. Hunters follow them. Who has the right to the animal—the hunters or the people in whose territory the animal died? Theoretically this could form the basis for dispute, but hunting bands usually form permanent alliances through marriages with neighboring bands, thus utilizing the bonds of kinship to avert quarrels. Since the meat of the prey will be distributed according to kinship relationships, everyone will get a bit of it, and fighting is avoided.

Once domesticated plants and animals become the subsistence base of the society, however, land becomes valuable. The efficiency of early and simple cultivation techniques is rather low. As successive plantings make the land less fertile, new lands must be cleared. This is a laborious process when one is confined to using stone tools. The River Dyaks, for example, live by cultivation in the midst of a hardwood forest. Their stone axes are barely adequate to the task of clearing the forest. So the River Dyaks cruise the river in their canoes, waiting to hear the sound of stone axes on hard trees. Having located a group of people doing this, the Dyaks wait until the task is finished, then attack, hoping to win the newly cleared land. The people who did all the hard work fight to retain the land, and a battle or raid, if not warfare, ensues. In this context, warfare may be considered an adaptive technique. The winner stands to gain or retain the land for next year's crop.

In the same way, as food production increases, populations tend to grow to the limits of their resources. If techniques of intensifying agriculture are unknown, the only alternative is to expand into new areas. This often involves driving off people who are already there who tend to want to protect their investment of labor in the land. Again, in this context warfare is adaptive.

It should be noted that in most societies where this type of raiding is practiced, the ground rules for the fighting are such that no great numbers of people are killed or even wounded. Seldom is there the capability or even the desire to inflict damage upon property. Rather, the killing or wounding of a single human being is regarded as sufficient to enforce the society's boundaries.

Attempts have been made to show that warfare of this type is also adaptive in that it acts as a form of population control. This is debatable, since no great numbers of people are withdrawn from reproductive activity even for long periods of time by such warfare. More than likely, the interpretation of warfare in simple societies as the attempt to achieve limited and concrete goals is correct. Among the Maori, as a matter of fact, raids were carried out for most practical reasons. Since the extinction of the emu, a large bird the Maori hunted, and before the development of modern market economies, protein was a scarce commodity among the Maori. They lived in fortified villages to protect themselves against the raids of neighbors. On any dark night, men of a given village, followed by their women carrying baskets, would steal down the trails to the neighboring village. Their goal was to surprise the village and kill as many women and children as they could, butcher them, and carry them home in baskets to be a much needed source of meat in the diet.

In all the instances we have discussed, even among the Dani, killing itself is not a vehicle for pomp, bravery, or fervor. It is accomplished stealthily. There is no ritualized protection for non-combatants. There is a need, and the only way this need can be fulfilled is to kill someone, which is done as expediently as possible, with the least exposure to danger on the part of the killers. And the least number of people are killed to accomplish the designated purpose.

What happens to a society in which warfare, however non-lethal, becomes a way of life? Chagnon (1968), in his study of the Yanamamao, describes this situation very well. The Yanamamao inhabit the Amazon basin of Brazil. Chagnon states that sovereignty, women, and autonomy are the basis for their warfare, not the acquisition of land. He terms this "social circum-scription," a term useful in describing the conditions of shifting alliances and the combativeness with which each group maintains its identity. Raiding is constant among them. They have placed a high value on aggressive behavior. As a result, their social organization, within a village and among villages, is in constant flux. Quarrels are frequent, and villages explode in hostility, bud off and form new alliances. Sometimes a group of people is forced to leave their land before new land is cleared and planted for a crop. Starvation would result if they did not form an alliance with another group who will feed them until their gardens are ready, and in whose quarrels they enlist themselves. Social relationships among the Yanamamao are fragile, subject to rupture for causes which a more stable people would regard as trivial. Chagnon leaves the impression that the Yanamamao are breeding for paranoia. Suspicion and violence are the very fabric of the society. Can this be adaptive in the long-range attempt to humanize man?

As society's investments in land and technology to work the

land increased, so did man's ability to wage war. Most early historic wars were fought for the possession of land or for the income of those lands. Even now, wars are waged to possess colonies, which consist in lands, resources, and the labor to work them. In a later chapter we discuss the motivations of the most modern type of warfare. However, with man's growing technology, war became a more dangerous activity. Large numbers of people are slaughtered, property is destroyed, and natural resources, such as forests, are ruined, as in Vietnam and Cambodia. Concomitantly it becomes even more necessary for authorities to convince people there is a good reason to spend years away from home and families, to risk being maimed or killed, or to kill and maim other humans. This amounts to a condition not too different from the Yanamamao, in which there is always an enemy lurking in the bushes, who is always directly dangerous to the belief system.

Since man is a self-domesticated primate, he has the ability to unlearn maladaptive techniques. Modern warfare is maladaptive. Its weaponry is both too destructive and too expensive. The psychological cost is too high as well. Ways must be found to channel these men and resources into useful purposes. If we fail to do this, we will be defeated, not by an external enemy, but by ourselves.

# CHAPTER 10

# $E = m \times t \times r \times e$

The anthropologist is faced with the problem of trying to answer what appear to be contradictory questions. Since the time of Australopithecus, mankind in general has come to control his environment with greater efficiency. He has created larger and more complex social systems, and he has discovered and invented new and old "truths" about the human condition. Yet there are people alive in the world today who have little more control over their environment than earlier men. There are social systems, fast being overrun, which, though satisfying, are so simple they lack the type of institutionalization we find in others. And there are many societies in which folk wisdom passes for science. The questions may appropriately be asked: What constitutes cultural development? And why are not all cultures equally developed?

## Cultural Development

Let us deal first with what constitutes cultural development. The anthropologist is keenly aware of the dangers of measuring "progress." The very idea of progress has subjective connotations. Progress is often interpreted as improvement, and certainly it would be difficult to get even a few people to agree on what constitutes improvement. For some it might be a return to an older, simpler form. For others it would be development in a specific area which would not satisfy others.

Anthropologists have been caught in a web of contradictions and subjective opinions when they tried to describe progress. Obviously, it cannot be measured in terms of lack of superstition or bloodshed, because no society lacks for these. Nor can it be measured in terms of comfort, because one man's comfort is another man's discomfort. Harris (1971) gives us, for the first time, the means to quantify "development" and the means to define that loosely held term "progress." He does this by relating his work to White's earlier concept of *negative entropy* (White 1949:363).

Simply stated, White's proposition is that the universe is undergoing *entropy*; that is, energy is emitted by the sun, which is in the process of slowly consuming itself. We can regard this process in terms of an *ecological energy chain* (Odum 1967). Energy released by the sun is absorbed by green plants through the process of photosynthesis. Animals are the second step in this chain. They indirectly absorb the sun's energy by eating plants or other animals. Man, uniquely, uses the energy thus obtained to build culture.

The balance of nature has for eons depended upon the return of basic elements to the earth by means of bacterial activity concerned with decay. Man, through the mechanism of culture, is using energy at a far greater rate than rates of decay make it possible to return the energy to the soil. Moreover, man's intervention in the balance of nature is becoming critical. The constant destruction of vegetation to produce homes and factory sites is reaching dangerous proportions. The extinction of animal species must be regarded with more than sentimentality. Plant and animal life must be maintained, not only because they are pleasant, but also because they are critical to the stability of the ecosystem in which man is but another, albeit the most destructive, predator.

Man uses the energy he derives in the ecological chain to produce culture. Cultural development, then, is a process of negative entrophy, and cultures can be rated according to how efficiently they use this energy. White's "law" of general evolution simply states that through all time, man's culture as a whole has grown larger and more complex. The indications are that through time culture will become still larger and more complex, though we discuss this in more detail in a later chapter. Harris's contribution is to show that this complexity is a matter of the efficient use of energy, which is quantifiable, thus relatively objective.

## Computing Technological Efficiency

The enigmatic equation that heads this chapter is the formula for deriving the coefficient of technological efficiency in given societies.

E = total amount of energy used by a society within a given time, usually a year.

m = number of people involved in food production.

t = time those people spend at their work.

r = calories used by the food producers which must be subtracted from the whole.

e = techno-environmental efficiency.

Several statements must be made before we use these figures to distinguish societies. We are dealing only with techno-environmental efficiency, the amount of energy produced by the society. We may not, then, speak of "developed" or "underdeveloped" cultures, nor of "primitive" versus "advanced" societies, but we can speak in terms of high-energy-producing societies and low-energy-producing societies. There is the additional warning that this type of efficiency is measured only in the short term. Many people in our own society are concerned with our pollution of the air and water, and they fear we will shortly deplete our natural resources. If this happens, our efficiency will in the long run prove to be very inefficient. But in the short run, we do produce more energy than any society has previously done or than any other society is currently doing. Similarly, we are not discussing the relative comfort or esthetic qualities of societies. We are measuring only one thing: the ability to take energy from the sun and convert it into food. Let us then compare certain types of societies for their relative efficiency.

A typical hunting and gathering *band* is a small group of people, usually related to each other. Their means of subsistence is based on the collection of wild plants and animals. Anthropologists assume that this was the type of society in which earlier forms of man lived. It is also to be found today in isolated areas such as in the Kalahari Desert in Africa, among the Eskimo, and among Australian aborigines. Although the prosperity of the culture varies with the amounts of food available in its environment, such cultures are usually marginal and exert no real power in the world today. The formula for such a band is:

$$E = m \times t \times r \times e$$
$$23,000,000 = 20 \times 805 \times 150 \times 9.6.$$

The number 805, which Harris uses to measure the amount of time spent in food collecting, is currently in dispute. This figure is accurate for bands living in difficult environments. However, Lee and others point out that in more hospitable environments, the figure can go as low as 200 or 250. Since early man had access to easier environments, we presume the lower number to be accurate for him. It should be noted that the r (150) will be standard through all the equations given here, since it is based on the average metabolic rate of working people. The efficiency of a hunting and gathering band is, then, 9.6. The figure must be greater than 1.0, or the society would not be sustaining itself.

The next group we will measure is a *tribe* that practices slash-and-burn techniques of agriculture. Such people have passed through the Neolithic revolution but do not have techniques for maximizing agricultural production. This type of society was present in small village groups throughout the world after the Neolithic period and persists today in New Guinea, the islands of the Pacific, much of Africa south of the Sahara.

$$E = m \times t \times r \times e$$
$$150{,}000 = 146 \times 380 \times 150 \times 18.$$

Let us now look at an irrigation *state*. This type of society uses irrigation techniques to maximize food production. The great Oriental empires were based on this type of subsistence, namely, China and ancient Egypt. Today this type of production is used in some areas of the Philippines, and it may well be true of India, where manpower is used as a primary source of power in the agricultural process:

$$E = m \times t \times r \times e$$
$$2{,}841{,}000{,}000 = 418 \times 847 \times 150 \times 53.5.$$

According to this formula, the efficiency of energy use has more than doubled again. The total energy put forth by the society is very great. In terms of human comfort, though, it should be noted that people are working twice as hard as they did before.

Finally, let us look at the figures for *industrial society:*

$$E = m \times t \times r \times e$$
$$260 \text{ trillion} = 5 \text{ million} \times 1{,}714 \times 150 \times 210.$$

The total amount of energy produced by an industrial society is explosively greater than anything we have yet seen. The coefficient of efficiency is similarly quadrupled. But it should be noted that more people are working harder than ever before.

The greater numbers of people, the more time spent at work, and the nature of the work may all contribute to the unattractiveness of the society from a humanistic view. However, in terms of simple material efficiency, this type of high-energy society will inevitably prevail over the low-energy-producing societies wherever these come into opposition. This explains why hunting and gathering bands and the slash-and-burn tribes are now situated in isolated areas of the world. If the high-energy society decided that those remote areas were essential to its interests, the existence of those cultures would be at stake.

According to White's law of general evolution, cultures have gone from the less efficient to the more efficient use of energy over time. In so doing, they became larger and more complex. Inevitably, the more efficient culture has overcome the less efficient one. This is a statement of cultural development which is quantifiable and objective.

## Specific Development of Technologies

The second part of our question was: Why are all cultures not equally developed? Here we turn to the work of White's students, Sahlins and Service (1960), for their concept of "specific evolution." Although culture as a whole goes from the simple to the complex, each individual culture is a system that is adapted to its specific environment and its specific history.

This has been restated for archaeology by Clarke (1968) in his definition of culture as a system which, through time, passes through a number of phases, the number and order of which are dependent upon the history of that system and the influence of its environment. Once a culture makes a stable adaptation to its environment, unless there is historic impulse to change, inertia will keep that culture at the same level of techno-environmental efficiency. Cultures in remote areas, isolated from the larger world, can thus maintain themselves at the hunting and gathering level, whereas similar cultures, located in an area more subject to incursion, will either disintegrate or be absorbed into the larger industrial society.

New Guinea has, until recently, remained at the slash-and-burn level of technology. The Caribbean area has not. These are instances of historical forces at work. No amount of encouragement, Peace Corps visitations, or techno-economic aid will help the Eskimo grow rice in the Arctic. This is an instance of environmental limitation. If one examines the technological inventory of the Eskimo, one finds ingenious inventions that maximize the hunting potential. The Eskimo's technology is superbly adapted to his environment. He lacks neither skill nor industry. His culture is an example of a fundamentally sound and stable adaptation.

Cultures, then, differ from each other in that each is in a

unique environment, and each possesses a unique history. Each has had to adapt to selective stresses brought by these two factors. In their differentiation, each is a valid and respected entity.

## Cultural Subsystems

In order properly to study and compare individual cultures, the anthropologist must impose order upon the phenomena observed in culture. The anthropologist is fully aware that such an order is a result of his scholarly needs. A culture is a system made up of subsystems which are in constant interaction. We speak of a techno-environmental subsystem, a sociopolitical subsystem, and an ideological subsystem.

The *techno-environmental subsystem* is concerned with the way man gets his subsistence and how goods are distributed. This subsystem is subject to environmental selective pressures. It is the most rigidly selected, since the culture must feed itself in order to survive.

The *sociopolitical subsystem* is concerned with relationships among people in a society, and also with relationships between members of that society and members of other societies. The orderly structuring of relationships in a group is essential to the functioning of that group. Most societies structure social relationships in such a way as to minimize friction in internal relationships. Those relationships that are potentially most difficult are often ringed with etiquette which tends to blunt the potential for overt hostility.

The *ideological subsystem* is concerned with such elements as religious belief systems, value systems, art, music, dance expressions, poetry, and philosophy. It is in this subsystem that the greatest variety is found. None of these elements is rigidly selected, because none is essential to the survival of the culture. Therefore, cultures can afford great latitude in the expression of these elements. However, there is some selectivity in that art tends to be manifest in media the particular environment affords, be it stone, clay, or wood. In the same way, art forms and religious beliefs are expected to communicate values common to a particular culture.

Steward (1955) distinguishes the techno-environmental subsystem and the sociopolitical subsystem as constituting the core of the society, with the ideological subsystem considered as superstructure. In terms of the definition of culture as an adaptive mechanism, it is apparent that the techno-environmental and sociopolitical subsystems are more important to the culture's survival than are its ideological manifestations.

It should be stressed that change in any one subsystem is reflected eventually by change in the other subsystems. To the extent that these changes are accomplished peacefully and relatively quickly, the culture will appear stable. Whenever one subsystem remains markedly out of phase with the other subsystems, the culture will suffer from instability.

Harris (1968:634–653) in stating the position of cultural materialists, is inclined to view the techno-environmental subsystem as the "prime mover" of change in society. Service (1971: 15–16) decries the idea of any particular subsystem as having priority in this regard. The argument is not insoluble. They both may be correct. In a simple culture, where the subsistence level is minimal, food resources are scarce, and there is little margin for error, the techno-environmental subsystem would indeed be a prime mover. Any change would quickly reverberate among the subsystems, whether such change implied an improvement in resources or the extinction of the society. However, in large complex societies with greater resources, there is more latitude for change to be introduced at any level.

Examples of changes in one subsystem affecting other subsystems are numerous. Turnbull (1968) tells the pathetic story of Gabriel, a young African man who became stateless because in his society citizenship was acquired by rising through age-grades, each ascension being accompanied by religious ritual. When Gabriel's father converted to Islam, he prohibited the boy from participating in the rituals that would have accompanied his rise to manhood, thus depriving him of his citizenship.

In our own society, the expansion of our technological skills has brought a value system which has best been called "consumerism." Items of technology—cars, appliances, houses—are seen as symbols of success, the acquisition of which is necessary to an individual's well-being. Nor can he rest content having acquired them, because he must constantly get newer models in order to validate this status.

Conversely, legacies from our individualistic past constantly confound efforts to minimize inequalities in the distribution of wealth. The Horatio Alger legends live on, although the applicability of such legends to our time is questionable. As a society, we still seem to feel that every person should make it on his own, despite evidence that this is not always possible.

Again, although the potential for converting to nuclear power plants exists in our society, this pragmatic move is opposed both by the powerful fossil fuel (oil, gas, and coal) interests and by the citizenry, who associate nuclear energy with bombs and fallout, and mobilize to prevent construction of nuclear power stations in their areas.

In simpler societies, technological change has been shown to initiate changes in both the sociopolitical and the ideological subsystems. Eskimos are now, and had been in the past, a *monogamous* society, meaning marriage with but one person at a time. For a short time, they became *polygamous* (more than one marriage partner). This was a change in the sociopolitical subsystem. Also, for the first time the Eskimos, during this polygamous period, recognized the existence of wife-stealing as a crime. The definition of crime in a society is an ideological matter.

Let us see why these changes came about. Eskimo men are hunters. The garments they wear are made of animal skins which have been tanned by their wives, who chew the pelts to soften them. For a short period of time, the European fur market created a great demand for sealskin. A successful hunter could keep up with the demand only by acquiring several wives to chew his furs. So much for romance.

In the next several chapters we shall explore the variety of ways in which each of the subsystems is expressed, according to the society's level of cultural evolution. For these purposes we shall use Service's (1968) categories of social organization. These are *bands,* which are small groups of hunters and gatherers; *tribes,* larger units composed of bands linked together by associations; *chiefdoms,* units in which leadership tends to become hereditary and in which resources are not equally distributed; and *states,* complex societies in which membership is acquired by citizenship rather than kinship.

# CHAPTER 11

# Money Isn't Everything

The techno-environmental subsystem deals with the ways man gets his food, with tools and techniques he uses to exploit the environment and provide necessary fuel and food. In this chapter, the ways societies interact with their environments will be explored. We will also deal with the economics of various levels of social integration.

The anthropologist defines *economy* as the relationships among people which makes possible the distribution of goods and services in a society.

## Hunting and Gathering Economies

Traditionally, hunting and gathering bands have been regarded as the simplest, and possibly the earliest, form of human social integration. The band varies in size, sometimes containing no more than twenty-five or thirty persons, at other times joining with other such units for short periods to form a larger group of a hundred or more people. Such aggregates form and break up for cultural reasons. People enjoy getting together for ceremonials and social intercourse. However, after a time, relations become strained, and the larger group breaks up into smaller units, each of which goes its own way.

Hunters and gatherers have minimal control over their environment. Men usually form small parties to hunt game. They are armed with bows and arrows or spears. The women use digging sticks to forage for roots and edible plants. As a specific example we might use the !Kung Bushmen as described by Lee (in Vayda 1969). This group of Bushmen live in the arid Kala-hari Desert of southern Africa. Lee states that the economy of the !Kung Bushmen approximates the following conditions: "mini-mal surplus accumulation; minimal production of capital goods; an absence of agriculture and domestic animals; continuous food-getting activities by all able-bodied persons throughout the year; and self-sufficiency in foodstuffs and generalized reciprocity within local groups."

Living sites are limited by the necessity for staying close to permanent waterholes. The Bushmen forage within a twenty-mile radius of their campsites. Small parties set out to hunt game, and women, singly and in groups, forage for roots and plants closer to the home base. The Bushmen may occupy a camp for weeks or months until the available food is gone, and then they move on. Among available foods, the most desirable are meat and mongongo nuts. The amount of effort expended by the Bushmen is in direct proportion to the distance from camp of available game and nuts. But the Bushmen enjoy a great deal of leisure time. As many as four or five days a week may be spent visiting other camps or resting at the home camp. Although only a few members of the band may have caught the game, and only a few individuals gathered the nuts, the band as a whole shares in the results of the foraging.

This type of economy is called *reciprocity,* the giving of food or other types of goods without a definite expectation of return. We use this form of economy within the modern family, where children and other members of the family are provided for with-out any definite expectation of return.

Students often question how this system continues to work, given the human desire to get something for nothing. As Harris has put it, the problem of the Freeloader is present. The answer is twofold. First, there are social pressures, mainly shaming, which will be brought to bear on a freeloader. Second, such transactions have to be evaluated in the long run, rather than in terms of an immediate return. The freeloader may in the future contribute his share and more, in the way a child contributes to his parents' comfort when he grows up. In the absence of such institutions as social security, old-age pensions, or health insur-ance, everyone's welfare is dependent upon his status as a mem-ber of a family, and all possible measures are taken to keep the goodwill of others, since mutual support is fundamental to ex-istence.

Competition and hoarding are regarded by Bushmen as antisocial and dangerous to the welfare of the group. Although there may be knowledge of game or vegetation available, the group tends to hunt and gather only as much as it can use within a particular period. This is probably due to several factors. First, the inefficiency of the technology makes food-getting an arduous and often dangerous task. Second, "since everyone in a hunter camp must be fed from the food supply on hand and since no one can be refused, the constancy of demand tends to keep food inventories at a minimum" (Lee, in Vayda 1969:75). Methods of preservation are poor, and whatever is brought in to camp is consumed.

Hunting and gathering bands employ relatively simple technological devices. An exception to this is the Eskimo, who has invented some ingenious devices in order to survive the Arctic conditions. Among these are snowshoes, sun-goggles, dogsleds, and igloos. Most bands exploit the land mutually and share the proceeds.

### Subsistence Agriculture Economies

A different set of conditions was brought about by the Neolithic revolution, during which plants and animals were domesticated. Land and herds became valuables. However, land fluctuates in value, because when the simplest methods of agriculture are used, land is not permanently fertile. Also, herds fluctuate in numbers, with young being born and other animals dying. The potential for a stable food resource, however, led to a population explosion, which resulted in larger groups of individuals, or tribes. We discuss how this comes about in other chapters.

Let us examine here the most common technology used in early agriculture, the slash-and-burn method. In this form of agriculture, the trees and undergrowth on a piece of land are cut down during the dry season. This material is burned to get a good cover of ashes. The seeds are planted in the ashes at the beginning of the rainy season, are cultivated several times during the season, and then are reaped at harvest. Lacking fertilizers or irrigation, such a piece of land, depending on the climate, will bear rich harvests for two or three years, then will have to lie fallow for seven to ten years before it is regenerated.

Individual ownership of a plot of land, under these conditions, is maladaptive. In most societies that practice slash-and-burn agriculture, land is owned by the tribe as a unit. It is parceled out to individuals as their need for land increases or decreases. If you have had the right to work a particular parcel of land, but do not do so (unless there is a temporary reason, such as accident or illness), that land will return to public domain and eventually go to someone else. In the same way, animal herds are constantly changing populations. Herds are usually owned by the tribe and parceled out to individual families according to the size of the family. This process is called *redistribution*.

Redistribution may be defined as the collection of valuables at a central point and their disbursal to a group under the direction of individuals specifically charged with completing the transaction (Harris 1971:651). This is one of the theories behind modern taxation. There are two forms of redistribution: egalitarian and rivalrous. Under egalitarian redistribution, an individual noted for his wisdom and patience is chosen to be the redistributive chief. Annually, at ceremonies held to unite the bands that make up the tribe and to reinforce their loyalties to the larger group, the redistributive chief collects all the herds and parcels them out anew according to the needs of the individual bands. This process was carried out among the Reindeer Tungus, who inhabit part of Siberia, and among the American Plains Indians.

Vestiges of this redistributive system of economy remain among Indian villages in Mexico, where, despite the long tenure of private land ownership, village ownership remains in the *ejido* lands which are communally owned and the use of which is granted to people who request it. There are social and political considerations in these villages to reinforce the proper distribution of *ejido* lands, but these will be discussed at a later time.

Egalitarian redistribution occurs when lands or herds become a permanent good and when the technology is still too weak to ensure the permanent use of these properties. In order to maximize the group's potential in food production, what is valuable must change hands. But the attempt is always to equalize individual productivity, because the tribe is still lacking in coercive strength. Membership in the tribe is based upon kinship, and behavior is controlled by social sanctions. Divisive measures are avoided, because they are dangerous to the existence of the tribal unit.

The Nyakyusa, an African people, go to great lengths to minimize differential productivity. In this society, people start to plant at the same time and cease at the same time, thus hoping to reap an equal crop and avoid envy.

In addition, egalitarian redistribution serves a cohesive function as populations of a tribe burgeon and bud off. Each group that moves into a new environment may find new types of food. A group that moves into an area with a lake may provide fresh fish, or a group moving into a forested area may find acorns plentiful. Egalitarian redistribution makes it possible for the entire tribe to share in the benefits of the newly expanded food resources, and it minimizes the danger of famine through single crop failure.

### Stored Wealth Economies

As population grows and food production stabilizes, some groups are able to store some resources. These become a type of wealth and can be mobilized for various purposes. An individual or a group able to mobilize this wealth can use it for the benefit of the tribe or for their own aggrandisement.

In the Trobriand Islands, for example, people were monogamous and *matrilocal.* That means that after marriage, a man went to live on the lands of his wife, and he received his portion of the yam harvest from her family. The chief, however, was polygamous and *patrilocal.* He married wives from all parts of the island, and they all came to live with him. At harvest time, each wife received a portion of her family's yam harvest. In this way, the chief controlled a larger portion of the yams than any other man. He used the surplus yams to pay other men to build canoes and make ornaments, so that the Trobrianders could engage in a rather extensive trading ring with other islands. In this way, the Trobrianders exchanged part of their harvest for other types of food and other items of value to them. The chief maintained his position partly because of his activity in the implementation of trade.

Rivalrous redistribution often comes about when a limited amount of land or goods can be obtained and too many people need those resources. As populations grow, a tribe using the slash-and-burn method of agriculture cannot continue to expand. When this happens, by various means some groups will exert a claim on the existing land, and others will be excluded from direct ownership of the land. For this to happen, however, there must be alternative ways of earning a living. We are then dealing with a *stratified society,* one in which there are several occupations and where people engaging in these occupations may be differentially ranked in the society.

One of the better known cases of rivalrous distribution was the result of depopulation rather than population expansion. The *potlatch* is a ceremony that used to be practiced by the Kwakiutl and other Indians of America's Northwest Coast. When first observed (Boas 1948), they appeared to be behaving quite irrationally. These people lived on the Columbia River, where salmon spawn, and they were primarily fishermen and gatherers of wild fruits and berries. They also hunted during particular seasons of the year. Since their resources were rich, but only land in certain areas was productive, the Kwakiutl had achieved a stratified society with chiefs who ruled specific groups and "owned" fishing rights at particular spots. In order to fish from those places, one had to ask the chief's permission and usually give him a portion of the catch.

A trading post had already been established, and the traders encouraged the Kwakiutl to bring them pelts by paying them in blankets. However, initial contact with Europeans had decimated the Kwakiutl, who had no natural resistance to European diseases. As a result, there were many chieftainships open, for which the natural heirs were dead. At the same time, those who survived were wealthy in blankets. The potlatches Boas observed were huge feasts given by various individuals. Each person who arrived was seated in order of his social rank, and the host gave not only food and drink but gifts of blankets to each guest. The guests returned the gifts in kind, each trying to give more than he received. Eventually the rivalry became so great that men would show their wealth by burning the blankets, much the same gesture as lighting a cigar with a ten-dollar bill. Ray (1955), among others who studied this phenomenon, recognized that these potlatches were feasts given by various individuals who hoped to validate their claim to an empty chieftainship by exhibiting great wealth and generosity. They were literally outbidding each other, in their own way.

## Market Economies

With the inception of a stratified society, the *market* comes into its own. People who produce particular goods need to exchange their products for others they do not produce. Although this can be done by exchanging commodities, and indeed many people still use this form of marketing, it can be more conveniently done through the use of money. Most people have some form of valuables that can be used for special purposes. For example, in some parts of Africa it was customary to give cattle to the family of the bride to celebrate a marital alliance. In some parts of the Pacific, pigs are used for this purpose. In the Solomon Islands, people used beautiful money made of red parrot feathers stuck into a rubber-like belt. Dogs' teeth, shell bracelets, and tobacco have all been used as money.

All-purpose coinage came into being with the development of the state. The head of the state guaranteed the weight of the gold or silver coins used in the exchange of goods, and to show this he stamped each weight with his seal.

Modern society is largely based upon a market economy, although we retain reciprocity within the family and use taxation as a form of redistribution. Modern money is distinguished by several characteristics. For one thing it is all-purpose—it can be used to buy anything that is for sale. It is divisible into smaller units. It is portable, unlike money on the island of Yap, for example, which consists of huge circular stones with a large hole in the center. This is special-purpose money, in that large stones are equivalent to a statement of the relative wealth of the family, and they are not used in everyday transactions. Modern money is anonymous. Theoretically, any person with the correct amount of money can buy any saleable item. In actuality, societies often place restrictions based upon age, sex, or race on the purchase of certain commodities and services. Finally, money is legal, backed by whatever state has issued it. We are all aware of the efforts to distinguish counterfeit money from legal money. The difference lies not in color or texture, but merely in the fact that one is endorsed, and the other is not.

Money is also a symbolic statement. This particularly is true in modern nations where coins and certainly paper money represent no more than an agreement in faith between a people and its government and between one government and another. The days of gold and silver coins that weighed a particular amount are long gone. In fact, the use of money is becoming less frequent in our society, where credit cards and charge accounts are ever more being used. Nations have long ceased transacting business with cash.

Markets can be divided into two categories: internal markets and external markets. Internal markets occur at stated intervals in various villages and towns. Peasant markets, which today can be found throughout the towns of Mexico and South America and wherever a peasantry still exists, deal in everyday commodities. Quite often, in parts of the Caribbean and Africa, the main marketers are women. They sell the produce of their farms, as well as their handicrafts. Cooked food is also a part of such a market. Shoppers pay in coins, paper money, and occasionally barter other products. Where barter occurs, it must be distinguished from the exchange of commodities among tribesmen and in bands. In tribes and bands, exchange of produce is seen as gift-giving and is not quantified. Barter in the market is based on the value of the objects exchanged, and although money is not exchanged, the monetary value of the goods formulates the basis of the exchange.

Such internal markets are particularly important in areas where there is a marked differentiation of climate zones, leading to crop differentiation. In North Africa, for example, city dwellers produce essentials needed by nomads of the desert. So vital is the exchange of goods between nomads and city dwellers that markets must be held despite the feuds which continually disrupt the area (Polanyi, et al. 1957). A man is selected to head a force of soldiers whose duty it is to keep peace in the market. City walls have narrow gates where entering nomads are stopped. They must leave their weapons outside. The peace of the market must be assured.

In Haiti, too, stalls are rented to marketing women who come to the city to sell their goods. The rent not only assures them a stall, it also assures them protection against anyone who might demand their space or disrupt the orderly process of trading.

External markets are conducted from ports of trade (Polanyi, et al. 1957). This trade is between nations, and involves luxury or state items such as gold, ivory, slaves, or other luxury goods. The port of trade is an international neutral zone, into which each nation can freely send its citizens without fear of attack. Often, such ports of trade contain compounds wherein reside the diplomats and soldiers of the various nations, sent there to transact business. The individual traders often represent their governments and use letters of credit rather than money. Shanghai was such a port of trade, and to some extent Hong Kong is still such a port. Other ports of trade were located on the African Ivory Coast and on the shores of the Caribbean in Mexico. The ports of trade were neutral areas where business was transacted despite hostilities between nations trading in the area. The actual trading was done by diplomats, men skilled in stating their nation's case to other nations. It was thus possible to negotiate peace treaties or to plot war alliances on neutral grounds. Trade quickly opened a path for other activities.

This kind of thing occurs in our time, as well, with such entities as the European Common Market which seems ready to attempt some limited political ties as well as economic bonds. This trend will be discussed at a later time.

# CHAPTER 12

# What Has Become of the Family?

Most people in our society are aware of the changing nature of marriage in our time. Divorce has become relatively easy to get in many states, and people seem to take advantage of that fact more readily. However, too many of us think that our particular form of marriage is somehow "natural." We envision it as the only possible form of tie between men and women. Let us look first at some of the purposes of marriage, and at some of the ways other societies have found to serve these purposes.

### Functions of Marriage

Most social scientists will agree that marriage has the following functions: *reproduction, enculturation* of the young, *security* for all members, a *division of labor* among family members, and the *linking of families* through marriage.

In looking at this list, we are immediately aware of the fact that many of these tasks are performed by institutions unrelated to families, in our society. Reproduction is still recognized as a function of the family. However, fewer years are given to this function, as smaller families become more prevalent in a society conscious of population pressures. Expanding nations or high infant mortality rates require large families. Western society no longer does.

Enculturation of children today takes place in day-care centers, nursery schools, elementary and secondary schools, and even camps that pick up where schools leave off.

Security in illness is found in hospitals, and in old age security is sought in old age pensions, Social Security, and retirement villages. The emotional and economic security of our children is often threatened by the fragility of the type of marriage we have.

There is little left of old divisions of family labor. With the advent of laundromats and TV dinners, men can and do manage quite well without wives. Modern technology is such that many women can and do achieve economic security apart from their husbands.

Few societies today consciously attempt to unite with other families by way of the marriage bond. When royalty was important in Europe, royal marriages were planned for just this purpose. Henry VIII, who had six different wives, was probably less a sex fiend than a victim of changing world policies necessitating changing British alliances. This may have been the case also with Solomon of the hundred wives.

## Marriage Systems

But it was not always so. For early man, and still today in band societies, each of these purposes can best be filled by marriage. But what kind of marriage suits the purpose best? There are two types of families recognized by social scientists: the *nuclear family* and the *extended family*. We have a nuclear family system. This consists of a man and his wife and their children who have not reached marriageable age. We share this form of marriage with the Eskimos, and for much the same reasons, as we shall see.

The other form of marriage, the extended family, is by far the most prevalent outside of Western European society. A marriage can be extended in several ways. The first way is *polygamy* which exists in two forms: when a man has several wives, this is termed *polygyny*, *polyandry* occurs when a woman has several husbands, but this form is relatively rare. Polygamy, though it seems strange to us, is extremely adaptive in societies in which there is much labor to be done and the population needs to expand. A man can obviously reproduce more than one child in nine months if he has several wives. Also, where several wives share the daily tasks, these tasks are easier and faster to perform.

Another way of extending the family is through the *joint family*, in which brothers live together, bringing their wives into the home the brothers share with their father. These people form a *patrilineage,* and reside *patrilocally.* The opposite of this is the *matrilineage,* which usually resides *matrilocally;* that is, women who are sisters continue to reside with their mother and bring their husbands into their home.

Usually the way people reside is determined by how they earn their living. Where men hunt or herd animals, the society tends to be patrilineal and patrilocal. Even where subsistence depends upon the horticultural activities of women, societies tend to be patrilineal and patrilocal. However, in some small confined areas, under conditions where women provide the bulk of subsistence through horticultural activities, societies are matrilocal and matrilineal. This may be seen in some parts of the American Southwest and some islands of the Pacific, among other places. This should not be confused with *matriarchy,* which means women rule it. In a matrilineal society, the mother's brother wields authority, not mother or her husband. Anthropologists know of no society which is a matriarchy.

## Joint or Extended Families

Let us look at the advantages of the joint or extended family in terms of the purposes of marriage as stated. Reproduction continues unhampered and may even be enhanced under a polygamous system, allowing one man to reproduce many more children than if he had only one wife. Enculturation of children is in the hands of more than just a single pair of people, thus allowing development of skills the biological parents may not have. The child also receives more adult attention, because there is usually some adult available even if the parents are not.

Security is greater for all concerned, a larger group being able to take care of its young, ill, and aged more readily. The children are not threatened by disaster at the loss of a parent through death or divorce, for the child will continue as part of a group which contains other fathers, other mothers, and other children. The biological parents are more secure, too, in that they can leave their children safely in the home place, knowing they are cared for.

And, in small societies, marriage is seen as the only lasting way of creating bonds among families. Thus bands marry their women into neighboring bands and take neighbors' sisters as wives, because in so doing they have mutual grandchildren, a tie that lasts for more than a generation. When a hunting band follows its game into another band's territory, there is no need for a bloody war when the other band is related and one can invoke the ties of kinship to make the incursion legitimate.

Many anthropologists see this function of uniting families as the main reason for the incest taboos that are prevalent in most societies. *Incest* is differently defined in various societies. It always means the marriage of two related people, but the degree of relationship differs from society to society. A *taboo* is a negative sanction prohibiting an act by natural or supernatural means. As White has put it, "Marry out or die out." If small enclaves of families do not marry outsiders and create alliances, they will be at a disadvantage, outnumbered by the larger affiliated families. They will be in a perpetual state of rivalry with other bands, with no way of stabilizing relationships permanently. Laws against incest force people to seek their mates outside their own groups, however these may be defined.

It may be surprising to learn that incest laws differ from society to society and are not necessarily based on biological criteria at all. In the joint families mentioned above, all children reared in the same home call each other "sister" and "brother," as they call all male residents of their father's generation "father," and all resident women of the mother's generation "mother." These children will not marry each other, because this will be regarded as incest; however, they will be allowed to marry father's sisters' children, because these are not resident with the same group.

Some reasons we usually think of for incest prohibitions are unfounded. Some people think that by close interbreeding, harmful traits are brought out. There are several reasons this is considered untrue. For one thing, inbreeding tends to bring out whatever traits exist in the gene pool; thus if a family has "good" characteristics, inbreeding will bring them out, just as it does in cattle, dogs, or poultry. Another thing is that harmful traits that occur later in life would hardly be ascribed, in a simple society, to a breeding pattern. More likely, it is ascribed to sin or bad luck or witchcraft. Finally, there is surely no biological difference between marrying father's sister's child and marrying father's brother's child, yet in some societies one is allowable, the other is not.

Incest laws are not only important for tying families together, but they are also important because if incest were not prohibited, the individuals having different roles in a family would still be the same individuals, so that the security, the division of labor, and the enculturation would rest in fewer hands, rather than more.

Joint and extended families, beyond spreading responsibilities among many individuals, also tend to offer more support to the institution of marriage. In earlier days in our own society and in simple cultures, families tended to select mates for their children. Often, children are betrothed long before they know each other or can live together. Mate selection is not based on romance, but on reality. The work of men and women tends, in simple societies, to keep the sexes apart much more than is apparent. A woman who marries into a patrilineage will spend most of her life among her sisters-in-law and her mothers-in-law. There are tasks she will have to perform to their satisfaction. She will be judged by the way she gets along with these people, how well she works, and how successfully she reproduces. At the same time, she leaves her family and its protection behind.

In many patrilocal societies, in some parts of Africa before they were modified by colonial powers, the groom usually paid a large price in cattle to the bride's family on marriage. The price was set according to the girl's reputation as a worker and her family's status. In all cases, the price was greater than a young man could pay by himself, and the price was raised by all the groom's kin. Upon receipt of the bride-price, the bride's father distributed the cattle among all his kin who had paid part of his bride-price. The groom's kin were buying not the bride, but the right to her services and children. In this way, it was to the advantage of both families to support the marriage. The bride who entered her husband's household was not merely the romantic conquest of the husband but represented a serious investment by the entire family. If she were seriously mistreated, she could flee to her parents, and the husband's group would forfeit the bride-price. If, on the other hand, she proved sterile or was returned to her parents for misbehavior or laziness, the bride's parents would have to laboriously collect the bride-price and return it. For both sets of kin, then, it was advantageous that the marriage work out well. A woman could count on the help of her in-laws if her husband mistreated her. A whining wife would be reprimanded by her parents. Every attempt was made to keep friction at a minimum. When the colonial powers limited bride-price, they did this because they equated bride-price with slavery. Actually, they deprived marriage of its soundest support.

## Nuclear Families

In our society and that of the Eskimo, monogamy and the nuclear family have been the rule. The Eskimo lives in a precarious environment. He has a nuclear family because he must be highly mobile. During the winter, he and his family hunt over the frozen seas. With the coming of the spring thaws, he must rush for shore. He cannot wait to gather up a household full of people, old and young, well and ill. He moves rapidly.

Furthermore, an Eskimo hunter can hunt alone. He does not need a group of men to hunt seal or to fish. To go whaling, Eskimos form temporary groups, leave the women at home, and work under the leadership of a whaling boat captain. On those occasions, sharing of the proceeds of the hunt is contracted by tradition. Most of the time, one man provides for his own family. In earlier times, old people were left to die, not because the Eskimo was unfeeling, but rather because old people forced to move rapidly alongside the dogteam could not keep pace with younger people. Their teeth were worn down by years of chewing raw meat, and they had no strength for the rapid marches necessitated by the ice breaking up. Dogsleds are not used to carry people; they are used to carry stores and equipment. The old people themselves often begged to be left to die rather than have to continue (Freuchen 1961). To slow the family's pace would have endangered everyone's lives. It was therefore necessary, sometimes, to build an igloo for the old parent and leave him or her there to die.

We, too, are a highly mobile society. In most instances, one wage-earner supports the nuclear family. Increasingly, rising in his profession or business means frequent transfers to other cities, states, and even other nations. Where both parties work, marriages themselves are endangered when one party must move and the other feels he or she must stay.

We have made a virtue of this necessity by teaching our children to be independent as early as possible. We cut family ties to such an extent that many children do not even know their cousins. It is interesting to note that in the less industrialized areas of the United States, where farming is still a way of life, family ties remain strong. In industrial areas, however, marriage has become unstable, and families are isolated from other kin. Although it is often believed that keeping a distance from kin prevents "interference" with the nuclear household, it should not be forgotten that this also means loss of physical and emotional support. We do not seem to resent our parents' financial support unduly, particularly if no "strings" are attached.

Mate selection in our society is quite random. People seem to choose their mates knowing little or nothing about them. Frequently, the bride and groom do not meet each other's families until after the wedding has been planned. Rarely do both sets of parents of the participants know each other. Given modern communication and transportation, people marry people from other regions. We believe that "love" will straighten out any differences between mates. In fact, the enculturation process, residing as it does in the nuclear family, produces children who differ in their ideas of how to do things. Many a marriage has foundered on the rock of variant modes of bedmaking, or handling money, or cooking.

There is an even more insidious process at work destroying our present concept of marriage. People are living longer today than ever before. In the course of these long lives, they experience many changes in life style, many choices in careers, many changes in themselves. A person does not acquire his personality at the age of seven and remain stable ever after. On the contrary, he continues to grow, learn, and change throughout his life. It is almost impossible to correlate one individual's personality growth with another's. For one thing, people differ in basic temperament; second, their life experiences differ. The young people who seemed to fill each other's needs so well at twenty may find themselves totally out of harmony with each other at forty. This is because they have changed, and their needs have changed.

Those who believe that the monogamous nuclear family is the only possible form will be surprised to learn that changing marriage customs are prevalent in most societies. Murphy (1960) studied the Munduruccu people in the Amazon jungle. At the time of his study, many Munduruccu were employed on rubber plantations, where they lived in monogamous nuclear fashion. However, in going back over the historical records of the Munduruccu, Murphy found that this phase was a relatively recent one.

Originally, the men hunted and the women grew manioc. At the time of their first contact with European Brazilians, Munduruccu lived in patrilocal villages. They fought the Brazilians but were, of course, defeated. The Brazilians respected their fighting ability and hired the men as scouts and warriors against other Amazon tribes. At the same time, European explorers demanded a large production of manioc, because manioc flour can be transported easily and can be mixed with water and baked or fried into a kind of flapjack pioneers have found convenient in the wilderness. The increased demand for manioc flour made it necessary for women to work together in groups. The men were away from the village for months at a time. As might have been expected, the village marriage residence pattern changed to matrilocality. With the new opportunity for employment at the rubber plantations, since the plantations provided housing for nuclear families only, this became the form of residence. All these changes were accomplished in less than one hundred years.

Marital patterns have been known to change in other ways, too. An African tribe in the former Belgian Congo was matrilocal and matrilineal, in which the mother's brother is expected to leave his share of the family wealth to his sister's son. He is also obligated to find a wife for his sister's son. Often this will be his own daughter, thus saving the bride-price. However, when the Belgians colonized this area, they introduced paid wage labor. As soon as men were earning enough money, they purchased brides for their sons, thus breaking up the matrilocal and matrilineal society, for a man now married his father's choice of a bride, not his uncle's choice, and he brought his wife home to live with his father's family.

### Kinship

In order to express various ways a society recognizes kinship, the anthropologist uses kinship charts. These are a kind of shorthand for expressing such relationships. Figure 12 is a kinship chart of the American family, a pattern anthropologists call Eskimo kinship.

In this chart, each horizontal line represents a generation. In the top line is father and his brother and sister, and mother and her sister and brother.

An unbroken line denotes blood relationship, whereas parallel lines denote marital relationship. In the top line we see that father and mother are married to each other, and each of their siblings is married. The triangle means male, the circle, female. Unbroken lines descend from each of the married couples to their

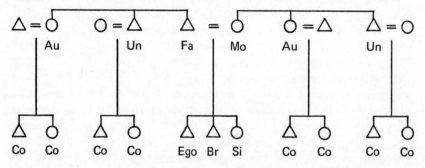

FIGURE 12.   A kinship chart of the American family (Eskimo kinship).

offspring. The second generation should be viewed from the triangle marked Ego. In kinship terminology, it is necessary to start to trace relationships from some individual, and we call him Ego. Also note that in kinship terminology, the first two letters of the term are used for abbreviation, so cousin becomes Co.

In this case, the older generation consists of people whom Ego calls mother, father, aunts, and uncles. His own generation is marked by a woman he calls sister, a man he calls brother, and other men and women he calls cousins.

The nuclear family is clearly expressed on this chart, because only mother, father, Ego, and Ego's brother and sister are given specific terms of reference. All women of the parent generation are lumped together as aunts, all men as uncles. It is apparent that societies which use this form of kinship do not have specific roles for these people to play vis-à-vis Ego. In the same way, in Ego's generation, only his sister and his brother are specified. All other relatives of this generation are called cousins.

In contrast, let us examine Figure 13, the kinship chart of a prevalent form of the extended family, Iroquois kinship.

In this type of kinship, father's brothers act as father to Ego. They may live in the same compound. In any case, they treat Ego as son, and he reciprocates by treating them as fathers. Similarly, mother's sister is treated as mother, and behaves as such.

Ego's father's sister, however, and his mother's brother are specified, because they play specific roles in Ego's life. The children of FaBr and MoSi are called brother and sister by Ego. To marry them would be incestuous. They are the children of his other fathers and mothers. On the other hand, the children of MoBr and FaSi are called cousins. In some societies Ego must take a mate from among them. In other societies it is merely desirable that he do so. Since the actual genetic relationship between Ego

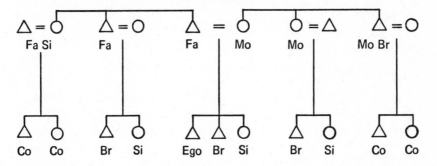

FIGURE 13.    A kinship chart of the extended family (Iroquois kinship).

and his MoSi children and his MoBr children is the same, we can see that our type of biological considerations form no part of the definition of incest in such societies. Nor should we be misled into thinking that Ego cannot distinguish his biological father and mother from his other fathers and mothers.

Kinship terms reflect social reality. In the extended family, father's brothers and mother's sisters perform those functions assigned to fathers and mothers for Ego and his siblings as well as for their own children. They are treated by Ego and his siblings with the same respect accorded the biological parents. The roles of MoBr and FaSi are defined differently in various societies. In some, MoBr has the function of finding a wife for Ego. In others, FaSi acts as chaperone and marriage counselor to Ego and his wife. Sometimes the functions are merely ritual ones. Among the Mesakin tribe of Africa, MoBr must induct his sister's son, Ego, into the age-grading society. In Ego's own generation, the numbers of brothers and sisters are expanded to include people we, in our society, would term cousins. If we think of the term "brothers" and "sisters" as connoting people we can rely on, people who will support us, we can see that Ego has a stronger familial base than that provided by the nuclear family. In our society, we often use the terms "brother" and "sister" to connote supportive relationships, without any biological foundation, such as fraternity brothers, sorority sisters, union brothers, and the like.

## Change in American Marriage Patterns

Are our marriage patterns undergoing change? It is evident that they are. As we have seen, none of the original purposes of marriage, with the exception of legitimate reproduction, are being fulfilled by the nuclear family only. It might even be asked why people marry at all, in our time.

The answer is to be found, possibly, in the increasing depersonalization of our society and the consequent fracturing of the individual's personality among the various roles he plays in this complex society. We are increasingly aware that we are social security numbers at work, an "occupant" as receivers of mail. A person encounters large, faceless industries in his activities as a consumer, where a person quickly becomes a credit card number. As we move from place to place, we forsake old friends and make new ones. There is a tendency to call a friend anyone with whom we have been associated for several days.

Yet, humans have a constant need to know and be known as individuals, as themselves, rather than as customers, students, teachers, or bowlers. There is the constant desire to relate fully to others. Having left parents and siblings behind, the quest for a mate is often based upon this kind of need. It can, if you wish, be called "love." Ours is the first time in man's long history that man must, if he marries, do so with none of the traditional supports which marriage receives in other societies. Given this criterion in choice of a mate, and given the lack of supports for marriage, and given the continuing growth and changing needs of individuals, it is to be expected that our marriages are relatively easily broken.

Today people are experimenting with living arrangements that do not necessarily include the ceremony of marriage. There are communes that link people of the same sex, and communes that include members of both sexes. There are newly created extended families, made up of couples whose bonds are those of friendship rather than kinship. Others prefer the more traditional one-to-one relationship but without the legalities of formal marriage. There are both advantages and disadvantages to this type of arrangement. The disadvantage lies in the fact that although the ties become as strong as those which exist in a good marriage, society often frowns on these relationships and exerts social pressures against it.

Margaret Mead (1970:163–184) has proposed that there be a two-step marriage system. The first marriage is a bond between people that can be dissolved at the will of either but is recognized by society as a legitimate relationship. According to Mead, this type of marriage could be tried several times, without penalty to the individuals involved. However, they must abstain from having children. The second marriage is to be entered into only after a great deal of experience and thought, because this type of marriage is the conventional marriage of years ago, in that it commits people to bearing children and to staying with each other for life.

It may be argued that in some sophisticated areas of the United States, these marital forms are already a reality. However, easier divorce laws have made serial monogamy possible in other areas.

Whatever marriage of the future will look like, one can be sure that it will be different from the marriages we are familiar with. Marriage based on personal needs, denied the foundation of economic needs, and denied the support of kinship groups is bound to be less stable. It will be interesting to see, in the future, whether divorce itself is so very traumatic to children. There is some doubt about the effect on children of mere separation from one parent, who is still seen occasionally. The trauma might be the result of the hideous infighting that occurs before a divorce and during divorce procedure when economic settlements are being decided. If this is the case, modern dissolutions of marriage, providing child support, but no alimony, and the elimination of the parasitic role for women should go a long way to ease the crisis. As divorces become more commonplace, the social stigma against them seems to have lessened as well.

Observations of college students today show a dramatic reversal of the roles of men and women in the marriage game. Not too long ago, women went to college to find a suitable mate. Today, more women are reaching out for careers, recognizing that even if they do marry and bear children, they will still have to fill a long portion of their lives with something else after the children are grown. Men, who used to try desperately to avoid marriage, are now the ones seeking it. Many young men find themselves at the middle or end of their college careers with no real idea of what they are going to do after college, afraid to face the demands of adult society, insecure, and torn between venturing out into the world and returning to the womb of home or college. Since they have been taught that they have outgrown their parental home, the only alternative is to find a willing mate and set up a new home in which they can hope to find security. These, too often, are the marriages that end in disaster, because the man will eventually find his place in the world and will no longer need the mother-wife. Before that happens, however, the wife may have found it impossible or uncomfortable to be both provider, mother, and wife to her husband, and she may have left. One cannot say whether these are bad marriages or good, because they do fill certain needs, for however short a period. Perhaps they should indeed be legitimized as temporary marriages, with no stigma attached to their dissolution.

However individuals manage their private affairs, they are going to have to come to grips with an increasingly complex society.

# CHAPTER 13

# What Is the World Coming To?

As technology becomes more efficient, and higher amounts of energy are used, population tends to expand. In fact, population tends to expand to the limits of the natural resources available to it. Anthropologists have found that this tends to be handled in two ways. The first is the simple process of budding-off. When the population becomes too dense in any given area, a portion or portions of that band will separate from the parent group and go into a new area. Most of the time, the groups involved maintain contact with each other and with the parent body through voluntary associations which we call *sodalities*. One type of sodality is based on kinship and is called the *clan*. Other types of sodalities are based upon ritual, healing, policing, or other functions.

This budding-off process is probably the way man originally spread through the continents. However, there does come a time when land becomes scarce. An expanding tribe often has to spread into areas already populated. It is under such conditions that Vayda describes warfare as being adaptive. Often a segment of a tribe, meeting fierce defenders of territory they wish to annex, will call upon other segments of the tribe to help them in their battle. In this way, the amount of force needed to dislodge the defenders can be obtained, but no more force than is needed is applied. A unit that can enlist the aid of its fellows can easily defeat a band that has no other segments to call up. When tribe meets tribe, however, the result may be a standoff. Since land is finite, at some point, the expansion must halt. Then another alternative may be invoked, stratification.

## Stratification of Societies

Anthropologists have spent much time and energy searching for the origins of stratification. Today, most agree that stratification can be defined in terms of unequal access to resources, and the causation is probably multiple. Fried (1967) speaks of population pressures, shifts in customary residence patterns, contraction of basic resources, shifts in subsistence patterns arising from technological change, and the development of managerial roles. It would seem that all these factors are concerned.

Primarily, the matter concerns the fact that with a growing population and limited land resources, some technology must be applied to maximize the productivity of the culture and, in this process, managerial roles are assumed by some members of the culture. This maximization can be anything from irrigation to trade or the use of a two-crop system of agriculture. In irrigation, some person or group must have the right to commandeer labor for the initial building of the irrigation system and then to keep the system in repair. The implementation of trade involves not only collecting the material to be traded and arranging for a meeting place, but also the maintenance of the "peace of the market" and protection of the traders and goods going to and from the market. The two-crop system of agriculture demands specialists who know when to plant and when to reap, because these systems are extremely dependent upon timing the cropping to wet and dry seasons.

These managers, and the society may have several types, allocate a share of the resources to themselves, not only to ensure their survival but also to reinforce their superior positions. At the same time, if the subsistence base is maximized, other individuals will be freed from agricultural labors to serve in other capacities as the technology requires.

Societies can reinforce the superordinate positions in many ways. In some societies, the ruling group assumes semi-divine status and becomes a privileged group entitled to special wealth, elaborate burials, and is protected by religious sanctions. In other societies, the ruling group takes on a military coloration, with special privileges which are preserved by force. The artisans and craftsmen who are displaced from agriculture are ranked differently in every society. In some, traders, such as the Aztec pochtecas, are ranked just below the nobility. In others, warriors or scribes may assume this status. In any event, a stratified society is based upon differential ranking of occupations, with classes having differential access to resources. Sometimes these status ranks are heritable.

In India, the caste system is based upon ranking and marriage within such occupational classes. In our own country, classes are less visible, with the consequence that people may assume they do not exist. Most of us recognize ourselves as members of a vast "middle class." Warner (1963) years ago differentiated that middle class into upper-middle, middle-middle, and lower-middle, as indeed he did with the upper and lower classes. But even this is not sufficient to explain the state of our society today. A budget report of 1973 shows that the 10.4 million poorest families in the United States received less than 6 percent of the income of the United States, whereas the 10.4 million richest families received more than 40 percent of that income (Fried, et al. 1973:38–45).

Far from being a classless society, or even a middle-class society, we do indeed have an upper class elite, a middle class, and a lower class. We do not recognize our upper class because they are, as Harris has aptly named them, a self-effacing elite. The key to class differences is differential access to resources and differential access to power. It is easy to differentiate such power when it is wielded by a royal family or a military junta. It is less visible when it is wielded by men in "grey flannel suits" carrying attaché cases, who live very much like their upper middle-class neighbors, but whose decisions on the managerial level of international corporations affect the politics, the economics, and the safety of societies around the globe. These people do not base their decisions on broad moral issues, nor are they concerned with personal public acclaim. Instead, they seem to shun any public notice. They are the nameless technicians whose purpose in life is to maximize the profitability of their corporations, to expand their economic domains. Governments and people are not viewed as entities but rather as potential clients or threats to enterprise.

Only recently are we becoming more aware of the machinations of some of our giant corporations in the politics of our country and other countries. Yet, these are not evil people or good ones; they are essentially bureaucrats doing their jobs. But the power they wield is frightening. If one can work through the interlocking directorates of the various industries, not to mention the interlocking directorates of the Pentagon and the "defense" industries, one emerges with the feeling that differential access to power—a power-elite—is a very real threat to rational decision making.

To look at the other end of the continuum, the lower class, we must remove the blinders our ethnocentrism has placed upon us. During the 1930s President Roosevelt spoke of a third of our nation being ill-clothed, ill-housed, and ill-fed. Some forty years later, after a world war and a War on Poverty, a third of the nation is still ill-clothed, ill-housed, and ill-fed. When we look more closely at this third, we see that it is largely made up of minority subcultures, black, Puerto Rican, Chicano, and Indian. It is a measure of our blindness that until recently the extent of poverty was not recognized. It is still regarded by many members of the white middle class as being due to the racial inferiorities of these groups. Some individual members of the white middle class will point to the Irish and the Jews and Italians who made it in our society and use this as a measure of the inferiority of today's poor.

There are three factors which should be discussed in terms of minority groups. First there is the factor of visibility. The Irish, the Jews, and the Italians are all members of the same race, although they had different religions and ethnic associations. Once they or their children became accultured to the larger American society, it became difficult to identify them physically.

Second, the earlier migrants were much better prepared for the American experience. They were Europeans, and as such shared our culture. Most of them lived either in small farming communities or in small towns. The Italians and the Jews shared a mercantile experience which stood them in good stead in their new country. The Irish had the experience of being part of the larger English-speaking world.

Third, as we discussed earlier, America was at a stage of development that required unskilled or semi-skilled labor, small shopkeepers, and factory workers. The Irish built railroads. Jews and Italians manned sweatshops, factories, and the small businesses that sprang up in an industrially developing United States. Passage was paid for many of these people by employers eager to get them. Their acculturation was aided by settlement houses in ghetto areas to teach them the language, diet, customs, and dress of the new country. Higher education was open to them both formally and informally as spontaneous "culture" groups hired lecturers, theatrical and musical groups to entertain and enlighten.

How does this compare with the situation of present minority groups? For one thing, these groups have been members of our community far longer than the immigrants mentioned above. Consider that we imported Europeans to do our work rather than give the opportunity to groups existing here. The special conditions of slavery virtually prohibited the teaching of reading and writing to slaves. Indians were wards of the state. As such, education was available to them only if they left the reservations and went into the few boarding schools available to Indians where children were separated from their parents for a whole year at a time. The Pueblo Indians recognized this separation by holding ceremonies for children about to leave for school, and other ceremonies to mark their reentry into the Pueblo world. The Navajo met their returned children with complete silence, maintaining that silence for days until the returning children had the time to readjust to reservation life. It is only now that Indians are getting schools on the reservations. As to the Spanish-Americans, they lived within a Spanish-speaking culture on the borders of our society.

All three of these minority groups came from rural back-grounds. The blacks were forcibly brought here to labor on the large plantations. The Indians were hunting or farming peoples who were forced into a farming or herding life, often on the most barren lands, ill-suited to agriculture. The Chicanos also followed the rural pattern. None of the three groups were trained to par-ticipate in industrial or mercantile society, except at the lowest levels.

Finally, it should be noted again that all three minority groups are attempting to participate in American society at the time when automation and industrial empires are making indi-vidual participation exceedingly difficult. There is no longer any room for the itinerant laborer, the small shopkeeper, the crafts-man. Opportunity today is open only to people who have skills acquired after long and expensive training, training that is often withheld from members of minority groups.


### Colonialism

The "underdeveloped" African nations are often cited examples of racial inferiority. Most of us are aware that great African king-doms existed in the past. But many of us are not aware of the reasons why many nations in Africa and Asia are today slowly trying to work their way out of grinding poverty. The reason is to be found in the history of colonialism. In the heyday of European mercantilism, the European market had the means and the desire for certain luxuries which could only be obtained outside of Europe. Spices, sugar, rubber, copra, hemp, coffee, tea—these are but a partial list of the materials which sent European fleets around the globe.

In warmer climates where these raw materials abounded, Europeans founded colonial empires. The colonies were equiva-lent to the institution of slavery in the United States, in that the "natives" were regarded as less than human, as literally a work force. They were expendable. They were either uneducated or poorly educated, just enough to make them reliable servants. The economy of the colony, which had usually been a subsistence economy in which people grew their food needs on their own land, was transformed into a market economy with a major exportable crop. As long as this export crop was profitable, colonies were exploited. The revenues from these crops were not reinvested in the colony, but were a source of revenue to the colonizer.

During and after World War I many of these exotic materials became unavailable, due to the danger of shipping through enemy waters. As a result, scientists successfully produced many of the products formerly transported from the colonies. Technology made it possible to freeze meats and keep them without spoilage, making high spicing unnecessary. Man-made fibers took the place of cotton and hemp. The colonies became liabilities rather than assets. Unable to profit from their wares when the market allowed, they were now granted "independence" which had no sound economic foundation.

A transformation of the goals of the high-energy societies became apparent. No longer willing to be responsible for the health and welfare of the colonial people, European nations now decided that these nations could still be useful as a market for their industrial products. Toward this end, the former colonies had to be developed to a degree which would allow them to purchase industrial goods, and yet there had to be assurances that they would purchase their goods from the nation making investment in their "development." This is the meaning of foreign aid, with strings attached.

Thus, the coups in Latin America; thus, the puppet governments set up all over the world. The head of the government was a native of the former colony. Service (1971) terms such a person a *comprador*. The comprador was kept in power by the high-energy society, with the understanding that sufficient aid would be given to create a market and that the market would be filled with goods from the imperialist society. In Cuba, for example, the United States supported by force of arms the dictator Batista and at the same time created two major industries in Havana, prostitution and gambling, both of which were illegal in most of the United States. A Cuban middle class grew up around these two industries, and their wealth was channeled into buying American exports. In Djakarta, our relationship with the former dictator Sukarno was similar. We sent in shiploads of electric sewing machines, but there was no electricity.

Students often ask why the United States, with its ideals of democracy and its history of revolution against tyranny lately appears to be in the position of supporting reactionary regimes throughout the world. The answer is economics. We need a comprador whom we can buy. The poorer members of the former colony who do not become part of the new middle class are worse off than they ever were, even during colonialism. This is because middle-class development projects soon encroach upon the land, and the lower classes remain on a subsistence economy, often without the room to grow enough food. The creation of game preserves, noble as this may be for preserving endangered species, encroaches upon the territory of subsistence farmers and hunters and gatherers in Africa. These people become starving exiles in their own land, because the government is run and managed by an elite chosen and trained for the comprador. Often, as this gulf widens, people rise in revolt against the comprador and his government. In cold war parlance, this can quickly be labeled a "communist" revolt. When it occurs in an iron-curtain country it is often called a "bourgeois" revolt. In either case, it calls for intervention on the part of the imperialist country to keep the peace of the market. It is only seen as a war of liberation by the people themselves and by the opposing imperialist power.

With the spread of internationally owned and managed industrial empires into these developing countries, the potential exists for more frequent wars of liberation. It is difficult for the American taxpayer to understand these developments. He sees his money going into foreign "aid" which is rudely rejected by the third world. He sees "communist plots" springing up from his seed dollars. He sees foreign nationals who have been educated in the United States, partly at his expense, going home to lead revolutions and expropriate American industries. But he does not understand that his "aid" is not aiding the people but the industrialists. He sees the industry as bringing prosperity and "modernity" to an underdeveloped country. He does not see that this prosperity touches only a few, and the vast majority are pushed further into the morass of poverty.

### Subcultures in the United States

This fragmentism is also occurring within the United States. We hear about subcultures and counter-cultures and alternative cultures. Some hail them as the wave of the future. Others fear them as Doomsday writ large. What is a subculture?

Technically, a *subculture* is a submersed ethnic group or

class within a larger society. As a high-energy society expands, it tends to overrun other populations. Thus, in Mexico, the industrial state has engulfed large numbers of peasant and Indian groups, each of which maintains to varying extents its original culture. Attempts are made to bring these groups into the larger community, but the sporadic nature of these attempts dooms them to failure. Well-intentioned groups try to teach Mexican peasants to make pottery, something the Mexicans have been doing for thousands of years. But this modern pottery only has a market among the high-energy groups while they are in the vicinity. When they leave, the market goes with them, and the peasant is back where he started.

The nature of technology today is such that little can be accomplished by the hand-craftsman or the small producer of foodstuffs. In order for the peasant to enter modern industry, he must do so competitively, and this requires capital investment. In the growing complexity of modern society, the outlook for the peasant, the craftsman, is bleak. Harris makes the point that rather than stigmatize the peasant for his conservatism, we should wonder at his willingness to cooperate with the experimentation of his mentors.

## The Culture of Poverty

Oscar Lewis (1962:xi–xxxi) defined an entity which he called the "culture of poverty." Although he first identified it in the slums of Mexico City, the concept has been extrapolated to include the slum cultures of nearly every major modern city. The culture of poverty is the adaptation to modern society of marginal people, often newly arrived from rural areas. It includes all the elements which city people find undesirable—crime, wife-beating, drunkenness, child labor, child abuse, and distrust of institutions such as schools, police, and hospitals. It also includes less criminal but seemingly irrational behavior, such as the purchase of electric appliances on time payments, the acquisition of showy automobiles, the unstable marriages, the general level of noise and dirt.

In order to understand this subculture, we must look at the roots of the society and then examine the new environment in which individuals find themselves. The peasant village is based upon subsistence farming. Often, in Mexico, there are communally owned lands which the poor may use to augment their crop. There are bonds of kinship or *compadrazgo,* which is a fictive kinship, which enable people to cooperate toward achieving a goal, be it providing food or building a house. People must often walk great distances to their cornfield, and life is very hard.

But there are social efforts to ease the burden. The men in the family, who do the farm work, are the rulers of the household. A man who has many sons or who works a large crop benefits from a high reputation in the community. Also, the community works to equalize wealth. Anyone who is reputed to have had a good crop or a succession of good years is invited to become an honored member of the village hierarchy. In performing this duty, he must give at least one *fiesta* a year, providing food and drink and music for the entire village. Often peasants attempt to avoid this duty, which can deprive them of hard-won capital, by appearing poor and speaking humbly of their condition. Nevertheless, in the face-to-face community of the village, such subterfuge is unsuccessful, and the prospective majordomo is acclaimed by his neighbors and dispenses his wealth. People leave this society for the city because they are aware that for some, life in the city is easier, safer, and more comfortable. They hope that this will apply to them, too.

Once in the city, the illiterate, unskilled farmer finds no market for his only asset—his ability to work. He cannot avail himself of the various institutional benefits because these all require forms to be read and signed, and he is illiterate. His wife, however, can find a job as a laundress, maid, or prostitute. His children beg, steal, run errands. The once dominant father becomes the least important member of the household. He contributes nothing; his pride is eroded; he takes to drink and to violence against those who have pushed him aside. Thus, the rate of crime and violence rises. For those who cannot deal with institutions, banks are unreliable. One has to sign papers; banks are often closed when most needed; and poorly clothed peasants are not often welcome in such institutions. Better by far to buy a radio on time payments and be able to pawn it when need arises. The many appliances are simply forms of capital.

In order to survive in the strange city, the peasant needs attitudes and skills he did not need in the village. Cast among strangers, he has to redefine his place in the social order. This cannot always be peacefully accomplished. The family structure, so strong in the village, is undermined by economic and social forces in the city. Children, who quickly learn the local language and geography, retain little respect for parents who cannot make the successful transition as quickly. The culture of poverty is a very real adaptation for survival under difficult conditions.

## The Counter-Culture

The subculture that has been called the counter-culture, or the alternative culture, is another type of adaptation. The counter-culture in the United States is the group of young people (and some not so young) who have become strongly aware of the inconsistencies, indeed, the corruption and inadequacies of American policy. They have attempted, sometimes through apparently irrational behavior, to call attention to these faults, with the hope that they might be corrected. Disturbing though their appearance and actions were to many people, there is no question that the attitudes of the people as a whole were profoundly modified by the actions of the young in the past decade. Besides the end of the Vietnam War, one has to consider the impact of such people as Ralph Nader and his groups, whose attempts to confront the society with the results of industrial pollution have not altogether been in vain. Although the older members of the community still give lip-service to old values, they have been forced to reexamine these values, and that is beneficial, although it is doubtful if the "greening" of America will come to pass as foreseen by some.

Alternative cultures are socially rather than politically oriented. Again, groups of young people are dissatisfied with present forms of the family, of work, of study, of entertainment. They search for alternative ways to live. On the face of it, this is a valid undertaking. However, some of the young people involved have little knowledge of history and little understanding of style. The idea of communes founded on idealistic principles is hardly new. Utopia, Oneida, and the Amish are examples of this type of activity. In some cases, the community did not survive the founders' generation. In other cases, such as the Amish, the community isolated itself from the larger society, and can exist only under the most stringent internal discipline. With each generation, more individuals are lost to the larger world. In any case, these isolated groups make little impact on the larger world, and the life style so established becomes an oddity rather than a viable alternative.

Finally, numerous people leave the larger society not to search for viable alternatives but because they cannot cope with our complex system. This will in time become an even greater problem than now, as society becomes more complex still. Going back to scratching barren soil to eke out a subsistence, taking drugs to blot out consciousness of problems, and contemplating one's navel in search of oneself are not viable alternatives in our time.

Technology will not be turned around. The larger society will not go back to hunting and gathering. Rather, it has already coopted the alternative life styles by commercially producing "natural" foods, genuine gold-trimmed, fitted denims, and records of country music. No doubt society will have to solve the problem of what to do with such individuals or groups. Mercifully, it may just let them alone. However, in the tighter integration that will probably accompany growing complexity, this is not likely.

# CHAPTER 14

# Which Is the Witch?

For most people, the most fascinating subsystem of culture is the ideological and artistic subsystem. As stated earlier, this subsystem is relatively free from selective pressures, hence more latitude for human ingenuity is allowed. Thus, great variety is the rule among societies. But this rule is not absolute, because the ideological subsystem does have a function: it serves as a rationalizing and binding factor, and it integrates the people within the society around common goals and beliefs.

### Belief Systems

The belief system also acts as a system of social control in most simple societies. Esthetic expressions such as art, music, dance, mythology, poetry, and legends are interwoven as part of the attempt to communicate common beliefs. During and after the European Middle Ages, works of art and music were commissioned by the Church and served to depict the actions and set the mood of ritual observances. It is only in modern times that art and music have become expressions of the artist's or the musician's personal view of society. In our time, art and music must be interpreted to the uninitiated. This condition does not exist in simpler societies, where conventional forms are understood by all members of the society.

When and where belief systems started is impossible to know. However, as we have seen, possibly Homo erectus, and certainly Neanderthal Man, expressed certain types of behavior we would classify as religious. Burial of the dead with grave offerings and animal skulls placed on columns lend themselves to this type of interpretation. However, in saying this, we must be careful not to impose our definition of religious behavior on other people. Religion in our time has become so unimportant to the integration of society that it is easy for us to separate the parts of our system we classify as religious behavior from other parts. In other societies, it is more difficult to see where sociopolitical concerns end and belief systems begin, because they are entwined.

In the same way, even certain elements of the techno-environmental system are ritually involved. In simple agricultural societies the priests inaugurate the agricultural cycle, and the saints are invoked to yield a good crop. Certain prayers must be said when new enterprises begin. And we still have the quaint practice of blessing the fishing fleets and the farm animals at certain times of the year. How long has it been since the monarchs of various European societies had to be crowned by the Pope?

In general, it can be stated that expressions of belief systems are related to the environment, in that materials locally available are used. There is also a relationship to the energy-use level of the society. Band societies do not raise Gothic cathedrals, nor do they support complex religious organizations. Systematically, belief systems may be analyzed as containing three elements: beliefs, practitioners, and ritual.

Belief in the supernatural involves belief in the existence of unseen forces which, for want of a better word, may be called *spirits*. This generalized idea is called *animism*. All living things are seen as having two components: a visible body and an unseen spirit which enters the body at birth and leaves it permanently at death. For many people, the spirit does not die but continues to linger either near the place of death or in a special place designated as another world.

The spirit is often believed to leave the body temporarily during sleep. The adventures the spirit meets when outside the body are conveyed back to the body in the form of dreams. Often, people refrain from waking a sleeper, lest he be aroused before his spirit returns. Man's preoccupations with his dreams still exist in the form of Freudian psychoanalysis, not to mention books that interpret dreams for the individual, either in terms of predicting the future or giving him a winning number to bet.

Spirits may also inhabit, temporarily or permanently, inanimate objects, such as holy trees, streams, or rocks. It is not the objects themselves which are sacred, but rather the spirit that inhabits them. This can be extrapolated to include objects regarded by the society as having particular powers. Amulets, icons, and relics fall into this category. Although the supposedly more sophisticated religions tend to reinterpret the use of such objects as being merely symbolic of a larger belief system, the foundation for this belief lies in animism.

Belief in spirits can be personalized so that they become deities. Various societies believe in a single deity, others in many deities. Where multiple deities exist, each may have a specific area of concern. Often, multiple deities are ranked in a hierarchy in which one of the deities is supreme. Deities are often seen as restricting their concerns to a particular people. Many tribal societies have a deity which is particular to them, as opposed to the deity of a neighboring tribe. Deities may be seen as restricted to a given locale. If the people are forced to move, they lose the protection of that deity. It is this element which has baffled colonial societies in their attempts to relocate people.

Spirits can be good, evil, or neutral. Evil spirits cause illness, death, crop failure, and the like. Good spirits provide game, a plentiful harvest, or healthy offspring. Neutral spirits must be coerced or cajoled into helping rather than harming man.

### Religious Personnel

Religious practitioners range from the part-time functionary to the complex institutionalization of a hierarchy of religious personnel. The part-time *shaman*, who serves as the religious leader of the band, is an all-purpose functionary. He is seen as being in direct contact with the spirits and is often possessed by them.

In the early days of anthropology, many studies were made of the nature of the shaman, since his behavior appeared strange in European terms. He often spoke "in tongues" (that is, uttered incoherent syllables), went into trances, or behaved in other ways Westerners consider deviant. However, upon examination, his behavior is that type expected in his society. Lest we find this difficult to believe, remember that our politicians are expected to don Indian headdresses and kiss babies. A hundred years ago, damsels were expected to faint upon the slightest provocation, and they did. Shamans are recruited by varying methods, depending on the custom of the society. Among some societies, shamanhood is passed from father to son. Among others, one must recover from a serious illness. In still others, shamanhood is foretold by dreams.

As societies become larger and more complex, the number of religious personnel increases. *Diviners* are specialists whose business it is to foretell the future and to uncover reasons for illnesses, crop failures, and the host of difficulties which beset man. Since both good fortune and bad are attributed to supernatural causes, the diviner consults the supernatural both as oracle and healer. The means of such consultation are as varied as are the cultures of man on earth. Some seek knowledge in the entrails of sacrified animals. Some burn bones and read the cracks in those bones. Others throw bones, much as we roll dice.

Often, the diviner and the healer are two separate functionaries, the diviner restricting his work to foretelling the future, the healer treating the ill. People in our society sometimes wonder how the healer retains his position, let alone his life, when his cures seem so patently ineffective. As a matter of fact, they are not that ineffective. The healer often has a good knowledge of herbs and plants. Modern medicine has adopted several drugs from other societies. One is ACTH, which was used as an arrow poison in the Amazon. Also, many diseases are self-limiting and people do recover, often in spite of the doctor. Since the causation is regarded as supernatural, the result of the healing process must be supernatural as well. Finally, we are now discovering that many illnesses are psychosomatic and can be "cured" by making the patient think he is cured. Modern physicians don't have perfect records either.

In a complex state, the religious system shows a ranking that is comparable to that in the society. There are priests who, though often "called" to their vocation, are taught the rituals of their belief system. These functionaries are not seen as inhabited by spirits, but rather as intermediaries between their people and supernaturals. The priesthood itself may be ranked, as in modern religions, with various grades of responsibility (bishops, cardinals, etc.). In some parts of the world, priests are the only literate people and function as scribes. In ancient Egypt, physicians, scribes, and architects were all priests.

### Ritual

Ritual may be discussed within two classifications: one is the type of ritual performed for the society as a whole, and the other is the ritual performed for an individual.

In our first classification, sometimes called *rituals of intensification,* the well-being and unity of the group is stressed. Annual gatherings of tribal groups contain much ritual directed to the continuing fertility and health of the tribe. There are also crisis rituals, such as rain dances or special prayers and sacrifices marking the ascension of a new ruler and the death of the old. Times of famine are also marked by a community ritual or series of rituals designed to find and ameliorate the supernatural cause. Most societies have a community ritual to commemorate the dead and to placate their spirits. This survives in our society as Halloween.

Individual rituals, sometimes called *rites of passage*, are used to mark stages in an individual's life. Not all societies celebrate each stage, nor do all societies stress the same stages. Rites of passage usually contain three elements. First, the individual is separated from the group. Next, there is a process of education, both for the individual in his new status and for the community, which must also adjust to his new status. Finally, the individual in his new status is reintegrated into the group. The status changes that are generally marked are birth, puberty, and death. In the case of birth and death, it is not the individual who is reeducated, of course, but the community, which must be ready in one case to accept a new member and in the other case to close ranks around the loss of a member. Marriage is often celebrated as part of the puberty ritual, but in other societies it is regarded as more of a secular than a religious ritual.

The puberty rituals usually excite most interest of the public. Some societies have them for both boys and girls, others for one of the sexes. Separation of the individual or a group of individuals who are at the same life stage occurs. The time of separation varies from group to group. Instruction in adult roles is usually given by older members of the community. This ritual comes closest to a period of formal instruction, in that young people are instructed in the history and mythology of their people. They are often taught the "secrets" of the group. These are secret because they are regarded as mystically potent and, if known to outsiders, could be used to work harmful magic on the group. For men, particularly, often a test of strength or endurance is part of the ceremony. And usually, some formal way of marking the initiate is used, such as tatooing or incising some stipulated part of the body.

Birth ritual includes the separation of the mother and the newborn from society for a given period. This serves a double purpose. For one thing, infant mortality is so high in simple societies, the baby is not officially named until it has a reasonable chance of survival. Second, relatives must be prepared for their new status as parents, uncles, aunts, or cousins. In some societies, the ritual extends to the father, who after the birth of the baby is also isolated from the community; he is in some societies kept in bed and fed special foods during the "lying-in" period. This custom is called the *couvade*. The purpose is emically stated as the fact that the father contributes part of his spirit to the baby, whereas the mother contributes part of her body, so his condition at the birth is even more vulnerable than hers. Etically, it may be a means used by the man to publicly acknowledge his fatherhood.

Death, too, separates the immediate mourners from the community. The corpse may be cremated, buried, or left to disintegrate on racks in the forest. The corpse may be interred, and the bones may be dug up at a later date. The survivors may be separated for a short period or a long one. They may be required to remarry quickly or forbidden to remarry at all. In any event, society determines what their behavior will be. In some areas, the widow wears the skull of her dead husband around her neck. In the Solomon Islands, for example, the skull of a recently deceased male is placed in a carved ivory box on a post outside the house. Mead (1961:219–220) reports that among the Manus, the skulls are kept in the rafters and are presumed to supervise the conduct of members of the household. In many societies, the dead become venerated ancestral spirits who must be fed on special days of the year, because incurring their ill-will threatens the health and safety of the survivors. In almost all societies, the spirits of the dead are supposed to take an active interest in their families.

### Functions of Religion

Religious beliefs should not be seen as having no relationship to the society as a whole. Religion serves two important functions in society: it serves as a common binding force, and it serves as a method of social control.

Evil spirits are not usually seen as randomly mischievous. They can be brought under the control of individuals who use the proper methods. Such individuals are usually referred to, in English, as *witches*.

Some witches are impartial individuals who simply manipulate the supernatural to serve a client's purpose. Others are malevolent themselves. But perhaps the most interesting witch is one we would call a "white witch," who operates for the good of the group.

The Nyakyusa (Wilson 1951) are an African tribe who, until colonized by the British, were expanding over neighboring territories in an unusual fashion. In the time frame we will speak in, they have both cattle and agriculture. At about age seven, the young boys are sent out into the pasture to mind the cattle. They form what is technically known as an *age-grade*. From this time on, these boys will be closely associated with each other, passing through the various rituals and age-grade classes until such time as they form a new village on the former pasture, composed of age-grade members and their wives. The Nyakyusa greatly stress the equalization of crops by starting to plant at the same time and finishing at the same time. This is particularly important, because although land is held by the age-grade society, cattle are inherited through families, therefore inequally. Villagers, therefore, vary in their wealth and resources. For this reason, there is a strong sanction against secrecy and privacy in general. The village is held together by the concept of "good companions." A person who inherits more cattle must make a special effort to share his food and his life with his companions, lest he rouse the jealousy of others and factionalize the village. Should such a person take to having his meals in private or going off by himself, he will be visited by a "white witch," called by the Nyakyusa the "breath of the people." He will be warned that his behavior is unacceptable and that he must change his ways. If some misfortune befalls the village before the miscreant changes his ways, he will be accused of witchcraft. Few people so tried are ever acquitted. The British outlawed witchcraft trials when they colonized the area. As a result, the Nyakyusa no longer feel safe in their age-grade villages, and Wilson describes families on the move from village to village seeking refuge from witchcraft.

In this case, the "white witch" is, literally, public opinon personified, and the evil witch is the antisocial person. In most witchcraft cases, the accused witch has been someone who in some way was different from the majority of the people. A case has been made for the fact that the famous Salem, Massachusetts, witchcraft trials persecuted people who through luck or ability managed to live relatively comfortably, while most people were suffering the results of a poor crop year.

Witchcraft may then be seen as a form of social control, and indeed much of religious behavior is an attempt to control society through supernatural beliefs rather than force. The taboos which surround a chief may make it impossible to approach him or to touch any of his belongings. This prevents people from harming the chief just as much as it preserves his sanctity. Where the king or chief is seen as an embodiment of a god or a direct descendant of the god, changes in leadership usually occur either through the intervention of outsiders, as when the United States deposed the Mikado of Japan, or through palace revolts. Ancient histories and the Old Testament give us tales of fratricides, when one of the brothers either ruled or was the heir to the throne. Harem revolts also play a part in regicides, as wives were the only people who could approach the ruler with safety.

Bizarre as many religious rituals and beliefs may seem to us, they should not be regarded as totally maladaptive. Harris (1971:570–74) makes an excellent case for adaptability of the seemingly irrational sacred cattle of India. Since famine is a frequent occurrence in India, many people in our country feel that allowing cattle to roam unmolested through the streets of cities and villages is absurd. The cattle, we think, should be slaughtered and fed to the starving people. Harris makes the point that the distribution of land in India is such that farmers cannot economically invest in farm machinery. They depend upon cattle for plowing. At the same time, their crop yield is so poor they cannot support the animals they need throughout the year. By allowing them to roam and scavenge, they can preserve them for the next plowing season. Also, the sacred cattle provide dung which is used for fuel by the poor families of India. Were these cattle slaughtered, Harris says, famine would result because the farmer would lose his plow-pulling energy, the people would lose the cheapest source of fuel, and, in a largely vegetarian society, only a few would benefit from the meat thus obtained.

Since the ideological subsystem is less subject to selective pressures, and functions to maintain stability in the society, it often seems that belief systems do not change. In fact fundamentalists of all religious systems believe that revealed "truths" do not change.

In fact, however, even conservative sources point to constant change. The Old Testament, again, records the change in ritual from human to animal sacrifice, as recorded in the legend of Abraham and Isaac and the ram caught in the bushes. In some way, the polygamy of the patriarchs became the monogamy of the good Christian. When the Mormons tried to revive polygamy, they ran into all kinds of legal trouble. It is merely that change comes about more slowly and unevenly in belief systems so it often is not immediately apparent.

### Myth and Legend

Finally, as part of the ideological subsystem, there are the myths and legends which make up the histories and mysteries of a people. *Myths* are often tales dealing with the supernatural and explaining universal phenomena such as seasonal change, day and night, life and death. *Legends* are tales having to do with individuals, often of supernatural origin but just as often historical, who influence the life of a people. Anthropologists often refer to such characters as *culture heros*. The Mexican god Quetzalcoatl is supposed to have been the king who introduced the domestication of corn. In actuality, the Mexicans domesticated corn some 5,000 years before Quetzalcoatl's reign. In the same way, Prometheus is supposed to have brought the Greeks fire. We know that fire was used by Homo erectus. Legends, then, are stories about historical factors which are attributed to semi-/ mythological characters.

In general, as man gains greater control over his environment, his need for mystical explanations lessens. Rational explanation and science replace many myths, legends, and beliefs. But the need for faith and help continues to be manifest in newer and stranger ways. As more complex problems beset society, many more people are afflicted with the sense of being unable to cope with their problems. Wherever they look, they find only more men like themselves, somehow muddling through. In the last decade or more, we have had a rash of flying saucer tales and even popular books written about people from outer space who came to earth and left some strange monuments ages ago. Is there some wishful thinking in this? Are we really saying that we wish some more knowledgeable and more powerful beings would appear from outer space and help us with our problems? Are we searching for our new culture heros in outer space?

# CHAPTER 15

# Now What? Where Do We Go from Here?

Science fiction buffs have often attempted to look ahead to see what man and his cultures will be like in the future. Their visions have often been intriguing, and sometimes quite accurate, when one considers the science fiction of only a decade ago. As we have seen, social sciences do not have a high degree of predictability in terms of a particular culture within a particular time period. It might well be that prediction should be left in the hands of the fiction writers and practitioners of the supernatural. Yet, having come so far, it would be fitting that we attempt a look into the future as the anthropologist sees it. To do this, we must treat, first, man's biological future and then his cultural future, bearing in mind that the anthropologist is interested in man as a biological creature as well as a builder of culture.

Medical science has come so far in alleviating our ills, and culture has overcome so many of nature's hazards, that we tend to think of natural selection as no longer operative in man. We use spacesuits to adapt to weightlessness and diving equipment to help us breathe under water. We depend on technology to compensate for physical difficulties. Does natural selection still concern us?

Indeed it does, because natural selection continues to operate, and those very miracles modern medicine has made possible may yet give us some of our knottiest problems.

## Long-Term Trends in Evolution

Let us examine man's evolution in terms of the long-term trends already evident. Since evolution occurs by the cumulative effect of minor modifications, we must reject the view of future man being born with wheels instead of legs and having one large finger for button-pushing, effective as these might be. Instead, we have the reality of a trend toward progressively lighter and thinner bones. The heaviness of bone so apparent in early varieties of men is evidently no longer of great adaptive value. Cave roofs seldom fall on us these days, and we do have hard hats for construction workers. People with lighter bone structure may have the advantage of carrying less weight around. Or perhaps there is a mere absence of selective pressures for heavy bones, thus making lighter boned types viable. Whatever the reason, it does not seem likely that this trend will be reversed in the near future.

Processing of foods has made chewing less important to nutrition than in earlier centuries. For this reason, people with bad or poorly spaced teeth are no longer at a disadvantage reproductively. We see an ever greater number of dental conditions which can be cosmetically repaired. There is no reason to think that this trend will be reversed.

At the same time, however, the very success of our species threatens segments of the populations. Hamburg (1961:278–286) has shown that population pressures produce stress reactions in certain people. His work and that of more recent workers in the field tend to show that the human reaction to stress is the raising of the levels of certain body chemicals which mobilize the body for action. The adrenal glands secrete hormones which originally enabled man, through a sudden surge of extra energy, to fight or flee his enemies. Under the conditions of modern society, the pressures and tensions of living in a complex and dense population produce the same reactions, without the overt ability to fight or flee the problem. We are aware today that a progressively larger toll is taken of our population by such diseases as heart attacks, strokes, and high blood pressure. These conditions are all related to the progressive blocking of the blood vessels by deposits of cholesterol from these episodes of stress. In fact, heart attacks, once a disease of middle and old age, are occurring with ever greater frequency among young people. Once confined to males, heart disease is now on the rise among women as females leave the security of their homes to compete in industrial society. It would seem that certain individuals have a greater capacity to cope with the complexity and irritations of modern society than others. A new selective factor has been added in the evolutionary process of man.

Perhaps the greatest problem facing the future has been brought to our attention by geneticists. Medical techniques now make it possible to treat illnesses which once would have removed the sufferers from the reproductive pool. The result has been that as the population has grown, the proportion of incapacitated individuals has increased dramatically. The degrees of such incapacity vary from the individual who doesn't see well without glasses to the individual who can only be kept alive by complex machinery. One would have difficulty in defining the term "physical defect," for where some degree of malfunction can easily be remedied, it no longer constitutes a defect. Yet there are many conditions which require constant care and help from others to keep the individual functioning.

On the one hand is the humane reasoning that every human being is precious and has the right to a full life. Certainly, one does not require physical fitness to create a work of art or a scientific discovery. Our culture would be greatly impoverished if the contributions of people who suffered physical handicaps were excluded.

On the other hand, we are haunted by the specter of a society in which increasing numbers of the "fit" must devote themselves to the care of the "unfit." It is not pleasant to contemplate the evergrowing need for institutions to supplement the care given by parents, or to replace those parents as their severely handicapped children outlive them.

Nothing would mobilize the antagonism of anthropologists more, at the present stage of knowledge of human genetics, than the thought of any political or legal institution defining who should live and who should die. We are all too aware of the dangers inherent in such a process. Is there no alternative but to continue on our haphazard way?

It appears that there well may be. Genetic counseling is now available at many large centers. Young people contemplating marriage and reproduction may now consult geneticists who will be able to tell them what their chances are for having a normal baby. Even more specifically, it is now possible to test an embryo for genetic defects. Once this knowledge is available to the parents, they should be made fully aware of the nature of those defects, the treatment available, the nature of the commitment they would be making if they decided to have a potentially defective child. At this point, the decision as to whether to bear the child should be a decision reached by informed parents only.

They should be free to make this decision based upon their individual circumstances and temperaments, free from legal interference or public censure. Ideally, the future may make this climate of opinion possible.

## Population Growth and the Ecosystem

Finally, there is the problem of population growth itself which faces the future. Present populations are taxing the resources of the earth. This growth cannot continue unchecked without disastrous results. The availability of birth control measures would seem to make such growth unnecessary, yet we are faced with very real cultural problems. Most people who know how to use birth control measures are the very people who could probably serve as the best parents. In cultures and subcultures where disease, malnutrition, and poor sanitation make infant mortality very high, artificial birth control would probably wipe out the culture. As it is, the middle and upper classes of Western nations barely reproduce themselves, whereas underdeveloped nations and poverty subcultures reproduce at rates that threaten their ability to sustain themselves. The reproductive rate in India, for example, outstrips any gains made by the revolution in agriculture. Where it is necessary to have many children to do the work or to gain prestige, people will not willingly accept smaller families for the larger needs of society. If ever the onus of minority status is removed, and mobility into middle and upper class status becomes a reality for depressed segments of the community as well as for poor nations, the goals of middle class society, including having fewer children, may become more palatable. If you are assured of the survival of your children, you need to have fewer. When the children's education becomes economically more valuable than their labor contribution, fewer children will be desired, since education is expensive. As people can reasonably expect to acquire luxuries such as homes, trips, and boats, they will postpone and limit childbearing to the extent that it conflicts with other goals. Until then, however, any attempt to impose population controls is bound to be ineffective.

As we can see, man's biological evolution is thus hedged by culturally determined attitudes. Is there any long-range trend to be discerned in cultural evolution? In terms of general evolution, there would appear to be some. It appears that increased technological efficiency is a long-range trend unlikely to be reversed. This implies short-term ecological problems, but these are not beyond solution. According to the Federation of American Scientists, the current destruction of the environment in search of fossil fuels should be mitigated in the early 1980s, when a production model breeder-reactor will be ready for the commercial use of nuclear energy. Given sufficient initiative and proper funding, science can find ways to overcome many of the inherent dangers to the ecology of nuclear power plants.

However, most problems that face the human population at present are of a magnitude that cannot be confined within nation-states. Pollution knows no political bounds. Population growth and effective distribution of raw materials and agricultural products tend to be hampered rather than helped by political boundaries. One can therefore predict, in keeping with White's law of general evolution, that social units will tend to grow larger, more complex, and more tightly integrated. Just as we have seen the development from small bands through tribal units to larger and more complex states, we should not expect that the current nation-state is the ultimate in development. On the contrary, as our problems grow in magnitude, and as technology affords more intensive communication, one can expect a new form of integration to emerge.

This may happen in several ways. It may be that rational human beings may combine voluntarily toward greater economic cooperation, which may in turn lead to political cooperation. This possibility is illustrated by the European Common Market which, despite its problems, is evidently working toward a larger cooperative unit than the individual states which comprise its membership. Alternatively, larger units, presently composed of ethnic groups incompatibly linked, may break down amid much bloodshed and mindless cruelty, and, out of the ashes, newer and larger groupings will develop. This breakdown is now visible in the Middle East, in Northern Ireland, and in the United States. It is not as yet possible to discern how or where the newer groupings will appear.

The failure of the League of Nations and the relative impotence of the United Nations do not mean the impossibility of large international societies. Rather, the League and the U.N. should be seen as early steps in that direction. When the larger societal groupings do come about, it is unlikely they will do so in answer to moral imperatives or political needs. More likely they will emerge as a result of the growing costs of modern technology. Supersonic transport, for example, is so costly an investment that England and France had to pool their resources to develop the Concorde. In the same way, nuclear energy plants are beyond the capital resources of most small nations, but several of them might pool their resources toward such a development. Out of this initial economic cooperation, political and social realignments may come about.

In the same way, it is not likely that warfare will be legislated out of existence. Instead, the increasing costs of military weaponry, combined with the maintenance of an expensive military bureaucracy, will prove too expensive when measured against the benefits to be derived from limited warfare or the potential destruction of total war. Warfare, an adaptive strategy for an emerging agricultural society, is simply obsolete in terms of modern industrial society. Since the acquisition of land or people does not serve the goals of modern industrial society, the military machine at present serves only one function: to channel materials and men into a wasteful, nonproductive industry. This can continue only so long as the genuine needs of the society are not threatened. When they are, basic changes will occur.

It must not be assumed that basic changes will always come about rationally. Modern technology has made it possible for governments to exercise heretofore impossible degrees of thought control. Increasingly tight control over the media, the use of wiretapping, and computer banks of information contribute to the pervasive intrusion of government into the engineering of public opinion. In some societies it is doubtful whether rational change can occur at all.

Another trend is that as technologies and societies become increasingly complex, there will be more and more individuals who will not be able or willing to cope with that complexity. New technologies require the services of fewer but more highly trained technicians. New systems will have to be found to distribute subsistence to large populations who may not directly participate in production. These are the long-range trends and the long-range problems.

What can the anthropologist predict in terms of a single society? As stated earlier, the predictability at this level is weak; however, certain hypotheses are worthy of mention. Most of us have learned history in terms of the "rise" and "fall" of specific societies such as the Greeks and Romans. And yet we have postulated that culture is a continuum. If we examine the emergence of new centers of civilization, we see that each does not go through the whole process of inventing domestication, the wheel, and fire independently. Each later civilization builds upon the cultural inventory of the past. Much of Roman culture was based on knowledge of the earlier Greeks. The Greeks built on ancient empires. As each new power center reached greater population densities, each controlled larger geographic areas, and each was more complex than the preceding center. Why could not the original site simply become larger, more efficient, and more complex? Why do we see such shifts in geographical centers of civilization? One suggestion is to be found in the "law of evolutionary potential": "The more specialized and adapted a form is at a given evolutionary stage, the smaller is its potential for passing to the next stage" (Sahlins and Service 1960:97). As applied to cultures, this implies that the very success of a particular culture makes it less likely that that culture can evolve into a new stage.

We have said that culture is man's adaptive dimension. To the degree that a culture adapts to a given set of circumstances, it forfeits its options to adapt to other circumstances. Thus a successful culture is an example of an adapted culture, but one which may no longer be adaptable. The very commitment to specialization that produced its flowering prevents the adaptability to meet changing needs.

### Trends in the United States

In the light of this hypothesis, let us examine our own society. Two hundred years ago, the United States was primarily an agrarian society. Its geography was such that expansion into new areas was not only possible but necessary to the security of the new nation. Industrialism was beginning in the form of small businesses, small factories, inexpensive technologies. All these circumstances combined to provide a society in which opportunity for wealth and power were available to the individual who had the fortitude and the ability to strike out into new locations to build homestead farms or into new industries. Society rewarded the entrepreneur, the frontiersman, the pioneer, the innovator, the individualist.

The advantage to the state was enormous. Individuals opened new territories across the wide continent. Individuals built the foundations of industrial empires. Individual inventions and ingenuity helped to make the country. The adaptation was superbly successful. We grew rapidly in territory, in wealth, and in population.

The realities of opportunity in the New World caused a stream of migrants from Europe to enter the United States. Growing industry absorbed these semi-skilled or unskilled workers and turned them into assembly-line workers. The worthy goals of individual enterprise were fueled by a democratic system which recognized every individual's worth as a potential builder of society. The pioneer was encouraged through land grants. Protective tariffs encouraged rising industrialization; the path was smoothed before the individual who was ambitious. The legend of the rough diamond—unlearned and unlettered, independent and ambitious, the self-made man—was born.

Today, farming has been mechanized, and has become another major form of industry. Unskilled labor left farms and fields and streamed into the urban centers. Most of our population today lives in or near cities. And yet the agrarian myth persists. Government subsidies are supposedly paid to support farmers, when in actuality they are paid to large agrarian industrialists. But the cities are deprived of funds and are largely decaying under the onslaught of supporting the unskilled, the minority groups, the urban poor who constitute a large proportion of urban dwellers.

The myths of the pioneer and the individualistic entrepreneur continue to exist, though the reality is that founding any major industry today demands such a large capital investment that we have the dismal picture of government funding of giant corporations to save them from bankruptcy. Yet the myth of individual initiative is so strong that government regulation, let alone government ownership and operation, of such corporations is regarded as outlandish.

Government support in the form of oil depletion allowances continues, although it now merely encourages the degradation of the environment and hinders the rapid development of more efficient forms of energy production. The small, daring entrepreneurs have turned into conglomerate giants, and tax loopholes benefit the extremely wealthy few and perpetuate the maldistribution of wealth and resources in the country.

Growth and expansion have become statistical measures whereby the economic health of the community is judged. There is, in reality, no real growth, only proliferation. Giant corporations strangle evolutionary growth. Proliferation threatens our very existence, in economic and human terms.

The democratic concept by which every man's potential was recognized has become a quagmire in which every man's opinion is as valid as every other man's. Public schooling, meant to develop the abilities of all people, has turned into a factory catering to the mediocre horizons of both educators and students.

The rough diamond, no longer the self-made success story,

is now simply a rough diamond, fearful of the rate of change in his world, unable to make his mark on it. He sits instead before his TV set watching hours of trivia and violence. He mouths the slogans invented for him by politicians and advertising agencies.

The eager workers have become bureaucrats who seek at whatever cost to maintain or enhance their positions in make-work jobs. Fearful for their security, they blunt the economic gains to be made by effective and efficient uses of energy. Yet, who can blame them? The myth that the aggressive, bold and venturesome person can always succeed is perpetuated in the indignations and cruelties we visit upon those who cannot succeed. We regard this as a moral crime, although in reality, the economic structure of our society is weighted heavily against the individual. Although we subsidize both agrarian and technical industries, we rebel at subsidizing the individual. The mythology of our society holds that poverty is the result of individual character failure. Therefore the individual who is poor is a "failure" and not worthy of help.

Democracy envisioned the enlightenment and fulfillment of every individual's potential. But political democracy has nearly become a myth, as advertising strategies obscure the issues in decision making. The low level of public awareness has made it possible to concentrate power to extents never before realized.

As is to be expected, some of the stresses in our society have been recognized. However, it is too early to assess whether such protests as have occurred will be effective. The antiwar and antipoverty protests were largely coopted by society. Men in grey-flannel suits grew their hair long and sported beards. Bluejeans were fashionable for protester and dowager alike. The unrealistic goals of Woodstock were quite properly made into a rather boring movie.

Other forms of protest—crime, terrorism, violence—have met with cries for more and harsher police tactics, the arming of large numbers of private citizens, and the slogan of law and order—the natural response of a people seeking at all costs to maintain the status quo. Self-correction would demand fundamental changes in our ideologies, our sociopolitical structure, and our technology. We have, it seems, become too well adapted to conditions which no longer exist.

Will some miracle occur to save us? What will happen to our society? Will it emerge into new levels of integration, or will it sink into chaos?

Quite simply, the answer is unknowable. Man is the only self-domesticated animal. Culture is the product of man's creativity. Neither forces from outer space nor inner voices will provide answers. He who hopes to "find himself" will be disappointed. We cannot find ourselves; we make ourselves. Man's continuing efforts to solve his problems constitute the humanizing process. Success will never be achieved, because every solution to a problem brings with it new problems. Thus the humanizing process will continue.

To the extent that man respects his remarkable five-million-year odyssey, he will gain respect for himself and for his fellow man. To the extent that he recognizes his own remarkable achievements he will increase his potential for further achievements. To the extent that he recognzes his own responsibility for himself and his society, he can not help but strive toward a more perfect world.

# Suggested Readings

### General Anthropology

V. Gordon Childe. 1946. *What Happened in History*. New York: Pelican Publishing Co., Inc.

Marvin Harris. 1971. *Culture, Man and Nature*. New York: Thomas Y. Crowell Company.

Leslie White. 1949. *The Science of Culture*. New York: Grove Press, Inc.

### Physical Anthropology

Frederick S. Hulse. 1963. *The Human Species*. New York: Random House, Inc.

M. F. Ashley Montagu. 1965. *The Human Revolution*. New York: Bantam Books, Inc.

Sherwood L. Washburn. 1961. *The Social Life of Early Man*. Chicago: Aldine Publishing Company.

### Archaeology

Glyn Daniel. 1967. *The Origins and Growth of Archaeology*. New York: Thomas Y. Crowell Company.

Brian M. Fagan. 1972. *In the Beginning*. Boston: Little, Brown and Company.

Kenneth Macgowen and Joseph A. Hester, Jr. 1962. *Early Man in the New World*. Garden City: Doubleday & Company, Inc.

## Linguistics

Joseph H. Greengerg.  1963.  *Universals of Language.* Cambridge: The MIT Press.

————.  1968.  *Anthropological Linguistics: An Introduction.* New York: Random House, Inc.

Morris Swadesh.  1971.  *Origin and Diversification of Language.* Chicago: Aldine Publishing Company.

## Cultural Anthropology

The entire series of *Case Studies in Cultural Anthropology,* George and Louise Spindler, eds. New York: Holt, Rinehart & Winston, Inc.

## Anthropology in the Modern World

Elman R. Service.  1971.  *Cultural Evolutionism: Theory in Practice.* New York: Holt, Rinehart & Winston, Inc.

Margaret Mead.  1970.  *Culture and Commitment.* Garden City: Natural History Press.

# Bibliography

Adams, Robert Mc. 1966. *The Evolution of Urban Society: Early Mesopotamia and Prehispanic Mexico*. Chicago: Aldine Publishing Company.

Alland, Alexander, Jr. 1971. *Human Diversity*. New York: Columbia University Press.

Altman, S. A. 1967. *Social Communication Among Primates*. Chicago: University of Chicago Press.

Benson, Elizabeth P., ed. 1968. *Dumbarton Oaks Conference on the Olmec*. Washington, D.C.: Dumbarton Oaks Research Library and Collection, Trustees for Harvard University.

Binford, Lewis, and Sally E. Binford. 1968. *New Perspectives in Archaeology*. Chicago: Aldine Publishing Company.

Boas, Franz. 1948. *Race, Language and Culture*. New York: The Macmillan Company.

Bordes, Francois. 1968. *The Old Stone Age*. World University Library. New York: McGraw-Hill Book Company.

Boserup, Esther. 1965. *The Conditions of Agricultural Growth: The Economics of Agrarian Change under Population Pressures*. Chicago: Aldine Publishing Company.

Brace, C. Loring, Harry Nelson, and Noel Korn. 1971. *Atlas of Fossil Man*. New York: Holt, Rinehart & Winston, Inc.

Bronowski, J. 1965. *Science and Human Values*. New York: Harper & Row, Publishers.

Buettner-Janusch, John. 1966. *Origins of Man*. New York: John Wiley & Sons, Inc.

Campbell, Bernard. 1972. *Sexual Selection and the Descent of Man*. Chicago: Adline Publishing Company.

Carpenter, C. R. 1964. *Naturalistic Behavior of Nonhuman Primates*. University Park: Pennsylvania State University Press.

Casagrande, Joseph. 1960. *In the Company of Man*. New York: Harper & Row, Publishers.

Chagnon, Napoleon. 1968. *Yanomamo: The Fierce People*. New York: Holt, Rinehart & Winston, Inc.

Childe, V. Gordon. 1946. *What Happened in History*. New York: Pelican Publishing Co., Inc.

Clarke, David L. 1968. *Analytical Archaeology*. London: Methuen & Company.

Coe, Michael D. 1962. *Mexico*. New York: Praeger Publishers, Inc., chapter 5, pp. 82–93.

Coon, Carleton S. 1962. *The Origin of Races*. New York: Alfred A. Knopf, Inc.

Dentan, Robert Knox. 1968. *The Semai: A Nonviolent People of Malaya*. New York: Holt, Rinehart & Winston, Inc.

De Vore, Irven. 1965. *Primate Behavior: Field Studies of Monkeys and Apes*. New York: Holt, Rinehart & Winston, Inc.

Donoghue, John D. 1963. "An Eta community in Japan: The social persistence of outcaste groups." *American Anthropologist*, vol. 59, p. 1000.

Drucker, Philip, Robert F. Heizer, and Robert J. Squire. 1959. "Excavations at La Venta, Tabasco, 1955." *Bulletin of American Ethnology*.

Eisenberg, Leon. 1972. "The *human* nature of human nature." *Science*, vol. 176, no. 4031, p. 123.

Evans-Pritchard, E. E. 1940. *The Nuer*. Oxford: Clarendon Press.

Federation of American Scientists. 1973. Newsletter, February issue.

Fischer, Eugene. 1913. *Bastaards of Rehobothen*. Jena: G. Fischer.

Flannery, Kent V. 1965. "The ecology of early food production in Mesopotamia." *Science*, vol. 47, pp. 1247–1252.

———. 1971. "Origins and ecological effects of early domestication in Iran and the Near East." In Stuart Struever, ed., *Prehistoric Agriculture*. Garden City: Natural History Press.

Fried, Edward, Alice Rivlin, Charles Schultze, and Nancy Teeters. 1973. "Setting national priorities: The 1974 budget." Washington, D.C.: The Brookings Institution.

Fried, Morton. 1967. *The Evolution of Political Society: An Evolutionary View*. New York: Random House, Inc.

Fruechen, Peter. 1961. *Book of the Eskimos*. Cleveland: World Publishing Company.

Gardner, R. Allen, and Beatrice T. Gardner. 1969. "Teaching sign language to a chimpanzee." *Science*, vol. 165 (August 15), pp. 664–672.

Golding, William G. 1959. *Lord of the Flies*. London: Capricorn Press.

Goodall, Jane. 1965. "Chimpanzees of the Gombe Stream Reserve." In Irven De Vore, ed., *Primate Behavior: Field Studies of Monkeys and Apes.* New York: Holt, Rinehart & Winston, Inc.

Gorjanovic-Kramberger. 1906. *Der Diluviale Mensch von Krapina in Kroatien.* Weisbaden, Germany: C. W. Kreidel's Verlag.

Hamburg, David A. 1961. "The relevance of recent evolutionary changes to human stress biology." In S. Washburn, ed., *The Social Life of Early Man.* Chicago: Aldine Publishing Company.

Harris, Marvin. 1968. *The Rise of Anthropological Theory.* New York: Thomas Y. Crowell Company.

———. 1971. *Culture, Man and Nature.* New York: Thomas Y. Crowell Company.

———. 1972. "The riddle of the pig, the human strategy." *Natural History Magazine,* October, p. 32.

Hart, C. W. M., and Arnold R. Pilling. 1960. *The Turbi of North Australia.* New York: Holt, Rinehart & Winston, Inc.

Hayes, K. J., and C. Hayes. 1951. "The intellectual development of a home-raised chimpanzee." *Proceedings of the American Philosophic Society,* vol. 95, pp. 105–109.

Heider, Karl G. 1970. *The Dugum Dani: A Papuan Culture in the Highlands of West New Guinea.* Chicago: Aldine Publishing Company.

Heizer, Robert F. 1960. "Agriculture and the theocratic state in lowland southeast Mexico." *American Anthropologist,* vol. 26, no. 2.

Hewes, Gordon W. 1973. "Primate communication and the gestural origin of language." *Current Anthropology,* vol. 14, no. 1–2.

Hulse, Frederick S. 1963. *The Human Species.* New York: Random House, Inc.

Jay, Phillis C. 1968. *Primates: Studies in Adaptation and Variability.* New York: Holt, Rinehart & Winston, Inc.

Jensen, Arthur. 1969. "How much can we boost I.Q. and scholastic achievement?" *Harvard Educational Review,* vol. 39.

Krieger, Alex B. 1964. "Early man in the New World." In Jesse D. Jennings and Edward Norbeck, eds., *Prehistoric Man in the New World.* Chicago: University of Chicago Press.

Kroeber, Theodora. 1961. *Ishi in Two Worlds.* Berkeley: University of California Press.

Lanning, Edward P. 1967. *Peru Before the Incas.* Englewood Cliffs, New Jersey: Prentice-Hall, Inc.

Leone, Mark P. 1972. *Contemporary Archaeology: A Guide to Theory and Contributions.* Carbondale: Southern Illinois University Press.

Lewis, Oscar. 1961. *The Children of Sanchez.* New York: Random House, Inc.

MacNeish, Richard, Antoinette Nelken-Terner, and A. G. Coak. 1970. *Second Annual Report of the Ayacucho Archaeological-Botanical Project*. Andover, Massachusetts: Phillips Academy.

———. 1967. "Prehistory of Tehuacán Valley." In Douglas Byers, ed., *Environment and Subsistence*, vol. I. Austin: University of Texas Press, pp. 290–309.

Malefijt, Annemarie de W. 1968. *Religion and Culture: An Introduction to the Anthropology of Religion*. New York, The Macmillan Company.

Marshack, Alexander. 1972. *The Roots of Civilization*. New York: McGraw-Hill Book Company.

Mead, Margaret. 1956. *New Lives for Old*. New York: William Morrow & Co., Inc.

———. 1961. *Cooperation and Competition Among Primitive Peoples*. Boston: Beacon Press.

Mead, Margaret, Theodosius Dobzhansky, Ethel Tobach, and Robert E. Light. 1968. *Science and the Concept of Race*. New York: Columbia University Press.

Mead, Margaret, and Rhoda Metraux. 1970. *A Way of Seeing*. New York: The McCall Publishing Co.

Michael, Henry, and Elizabeth Ralph. 1971. *Dating Techniques for the Archaeologist*. Cambridge: The MIT Press.

Millon, René F. 1964. "The Teotihuacán Mapping Project." *American Antiquity*, vol. 29, pp. 345–352.

Montagu, M. F. Ashley. 1968. *Culture, Man's Adaptive Dimension*. New York: Oxford University Press, Inc.

Morris, Desmond. 1962. *The Biology of Art*. New York: Alfred A. Knopf, Inc.

Murphy, Robert F. 1960. *Head Hunters' Heritage: Social and Economic Change Among the Mundurucu Indians*. Berkeley: University of California Press.

Odum, Eugene P. 1967. *Fundamentals of Ecology*. 2nd edition. Philadelphia: W. B. Saunders Company.

Pilbeam, D. R., and E. L. Simons. 1965. "Some problems of hominid classification." *American Science*, vol. 53, p. 237.

Polanyi, Karl, Conrad M. Arensberg, and Harry W. Pearson. 1957. *Trade and Markets in the Early Empires*. Glencoe, Illinois: The Free Press.

Premack, Ann James, and David Premack. 1972. "Teaching language to an ape." *Scientific American*, vol. 227, pp. 92–99.

Rappaport, Roy. 1968. *Pigs for the Ancestors: Ritual in the Ecology of a New Guinea People*. New Haven: Yale University Press.

Ray, Vernon. 1955. "Review of Franz Boas: The science of man in the making by M. Herskovitz." *American Anthropologist*, vol. 57, pp. 138–141.

Reynolds, Vernon, and Frances Reynolds. 1965. "Chimpanzees of the Budongo Forest." In Irven De Vore, ed., *Primate Behavior: Field Studies of Monkeys and Apes.* New York: Holt, Rinehart & Winston, Inc.

Sahlins, Marshal, and Elman Service. 1960. *Evolution and Culture.* Ann Arbor: University of Michigan Press.

Sanders, William, and Barbara Price. 1968. *Mesoamerica: The Evolution of a Civilization.* New York: Random House, Inc.

Schaller, George B. 1963. *The Year of the Gorilla.* Chicago: University of Chicago Press.

Service, Elman R. 1968. *Primitive Social Organization.* New York: Random House, Inc.

————. 1971. *Cultural Evolutionism: Theory in Practice.* New York: Holt, Rinehart & Winston, Inc.

Shapiro, Harry. 1929. *Descendants of the Mutineers of the Bounty.* Hawaii: Bernice P. Bishop Museum.

————. 1960. *The Jewish People.* New York: UNESCO.

Siegal, B. J., ed. 1972. *Annual Review of Anthropology,* vol. 1. Palo Alto, California: Annual Reviews.

Sipes, Richard G. 1973. "War, sports, and aggression: An empirical test of two rival theories." *American Anthropologist,* vol. 75, no. 1, pp. 64–86.

Solecki, Ralph. 1971. *Shanidar: The First Flower People.* New York: Alfred A. Knopf, Inc.

Solheim, Wilhelm. 1972. "The earlier agricultural revolution." *Scientific American,* vol. 226 (April), pp. 34–41.

Southwick, Charles H. 1963. *Primate Social Behavior.* New York: D. Van Nostrand, Inc.

Steward, Julian. 1955. *Theory of Culture Change.* Urbana: University of Illinois Press.

Sturtevant, Edgar H. 1947. *An Introduction to Linguistic Sciences.* New Haven: Yale University Press.

Teilhard de Chardin, Pierre. 1959. *The Phenomena of Man.* New York: Harper & Row, Publishers.

Turnbull, Colin M. 1966. *Tradition and Change in African Tribal Life.* Chicago: Avon Books.

————. 1968. *The Lonely African.* New York: Simon & Schuster, Inc.

————. 1972. *The Mountain People.* New York: Simon & Schuster, Inc.

Ucko, Peter J., Ruth Tringham, and G. W. Dimbleby. 1972. *Man, Settlement, and Urbanism.* Cambridge, Massachusetts: Schenkman Publishing Co., Inc.

Van-Lawick-Goodall, Jane. 1963. "Life among the wild chimpanzees." *National Geographic,* vol. 124, pp. 272–308.

————. 1968. "The behavior of free-living chimpanzees in the Gombe Stream Reserve." *Animal Behavior Monographs* 1, 3, pp. 161–311.

Vayda, Andrew. 1960. *Maori Warfare.* Polynesian Society Maori Monographs No. 2. Wellington, New Zealand: Polynesian Society.

————. 1969. *Environment and Cultural Behavior: Ecological Studies in Cultural Anthropology.* Garden City: Natural History Press.

Wagley, Charles. 1963. *An Introduction to Brazil.* New York: Columbia University Press.

Warner, Lloyd. 1963. *Yankee City.* New Haven: Yale University Press.

Washburn, Sherwood L. 1961. *The Social Life of Early Man.* Chicago: Aldine Publishing Company.

White, Leslie. 1949. *The Science of Culture.* New York: Grove Press, Inc.

Willey, Gordon. 1966. *An Introduction to American Archaeology.* Vol. I: *North and Middle America.* Englewood Cliffs, New Jersey: Prentice-Hall, Inc.

————. 1971. *An Introduction to American Archaeology.* Vol. II: *South America.* Englewood Cliffs, New Jersey: Prentice-Hall, Inc.

Wilson, Monica. 1951. *Good Company: A Study of Nyakyusa Age-Village.* Boston: Beacon Press.

Wittfogel, Karl. 1957. *Oriental Despotism: A Comparative Study of Total Power.* New Haven: Yale University Press.

# Index

## A

Absolute dating, 71
Acculturation, 136
  defined, 11
  and intelligence theory, 57–59
ACTH, 147
Adaptation, 11–13
  brachiation, 42
  long- / short-term, 11–13
Adaptive radiation, 23
Agassiz, Louis, 4
Agriculture, 88–90
  intensification of, 88–89, 90
  irrigation, 88, 89, 108, 134
  site rotation, 88
  slash-and-burn, 108, 115
  subsistence, 115–117, 140
  surplus, 89, 114
  Tehuacán Valley, 87–88
  terraces, 88
Alleles, 50
Alphabet, development, 67
Alternative cultures, 139, 141–142
Altmann, S. A., 37
Animals, domestication, 82–83, 88,
    102, 115
Animism, 145
Anthropocentrism, 5
Anthropologists, 8–9
  and cultural development, 105–106
  as participant-observers, 14
  training, 13–14

Anthropology, 1
  holistic discipline, 13
  and linguistics, 67–69
  method, 5–7, 13–15
Archaeologists, 9
  techniques of, 71–72
Archaeology, 70–84
  and artifacts, 72–79
Artifacts, 9, 10
  fossil man, 72–79
Astronomy, interest in, 79
Australopithecus, 21, 27–29, 31, 42,
    72, 80
Aztec people, 94–95, 134

## B

Baboons, 37–41
  cynocephalus/hamadryas groups,
    37–38
  development, 39
  dominance among, 38–40
  reproduction, 40–41
Bands, 6
  defined, 112
Barter, 119–120
Basques, 52
Behavioral characteristics of
    primates, 36–47
Belief systems, 144–146
  Dani people, 101
  religion, 146–152

Birth control, 155, 156
Birth rituals, 148–149
Black Intelligence Test for Cultural
    Homogeneity, 57–58
Blacks, American, 52, 54–60, 136
Boas, Franz, 6, 118
Bohr, Niels, 2
Brace, C. Loring, 27, 31
Brachiation, 42
Brain size, 25, 28–29, 31, 32, 34
Breeding population, 21–23, 29
Bride price, 125
Bronowski, Jacob, 2–3
Buffon, Comte de, 2, 20
Bushmen, !Kung:
    bands, 6
    economy, 113–115
Busing, racism and, 54–55

C

Calendar, use of, 79, 93
Carbon dating, 71–72
Carpenter, C. R., 37
Casagrande, Joseph, 14
Caste system, 135
Catastrophism, 20
Cave art, 77–79
Ceremonial centers, 90, 91, 93
    Techuacán Valley, 87–88
Chagnon, Napoleon, 103
Champollion, Jean, 67
Chardin, Pierre Teilhard de, 21
Chichén Itzá, 94
Chiefdoms, defined, 112
Chimpanzees, 41–47
    blood types, similarity with man's,
        42
    communication, 43, 45–47
    development, 44
    display behavior, 97
    dominance among, 44–45
    reproduction, 44
    tool-making, 43–44
Chopper-chopping tool, 73
Cities, 85, 90
Civilization, 85–95
    defined, 85
    Mesoamerican, 90–95
    New World, 86–88, 90–95
    Tehuacán Valley, 86–88

Clans, 133
Clarke, David L., 109
Classes, social, 90, 135
Classification, fossil man, 29–31
Coe, Michael D., 91
Colonialism, 137–139
Communes, 131
Communication:
    in chimpanzees, 43, 45–47
    in man, 61–69
Competition, antisocial, 114–115
Compradrazgo, 140–141
Coon, Carleton, 33
Cortez, Hernando, 94
Counter-cultures, 139, 141–142
Couvade, 149
Crime, 112, 141
Cultural anthropologists, 9
Cultural development, 105–106
    and environment, 109
Cultural relativism, 16–19
Cultural selection, 24–25
Cultural systems:
    changing, 17
    functions, 17
    subsystems, 110–112
Culture, 9–13
    characteristics, 9
    cumulative nature, 9–10, 158–159
    defined, 9
    emic/etic views, 14–15
    and race, 49, 53, 58–60
    transgenerational, 10–11
Culture heroes, 152
Culture shock, 17–18

D

Dani people, 101
Dart, R. A., 27
Darwin, Charles, 2, 10, 11, 16, 21,
    22
Dating procedures, 71–72
Death rituals, 149
    of Neanderthal Man, 76, 144–145
Decalcification, 23, 25, 35, 154
Deities, belief in, 146
Dentition, 26, 31, 32, 34
Deoxyribonucleic acid (DNA), 49–50
Dialects, 64–65

Diet:
    baboons, 38
    chimpanzees, 43
    meat-eating, 38, 74
Display behavior, chimpanzees, 97
Distribution systems, 89, 158
Diviners, 147
Division of labor, family, 121, 122
Divorce, 121, 132
Domestication:
    animals, 82–83, 88, 102, 115
    plants, 82–83, 87, 88, 102, 115
    vs. taming, 81
Dominance:
    baboons, 38–40
    chimpanzees, 44–45
Dreaming, and belief in spirits, 145, 146
*Dryopithecus,* 25–26, 42, 97
Dyak people, 102

## E

Ecological energy chain, 106
Economic factors:
    colonialism, 137–139
    economy defined, 113
    hunting and gathering, 113–115
    markets, 118–120
    reciprocity, 114
    stored wealth, 117–118
    subsistence agriculture, 115–117
Efficiency, computing technological, 106–109
Eisenberg, Leon, 98
*Ejido,* 116
Emic view, culture, 14–15
Enculturation:
    defined, 10
    erect posture and, 29
    function of marriage, 121–122, 123
    and intelligence theory, 57–59
Entropy, 106
Environment:
    and belief systems, 145
    control by man, 105, 113
    and cultural development, 109
    and natural selection, 22–23
    technology and, 156–159
Erect posture, 29, 31, 42

Eskimo people, 16, 107, 109, 112, 114, 122, 125–126
Ethnocentrism, 16–19
Etic view, culture, 14–15
Evans-Pritchard, E. E., 18
Evolution:
    brain size, 25, 28–29, 31, 32, 34
    continuity of, 23–24
    decalcification, 23, 25, 35, 154
    defined, 20
    long-term trends, 154–156, 159–162
    natural selection, 21–23
    White's law of, 6–7, 109, 157
Evolutionary potential, law of, 159
Extended family, 122, 123–125
    kinship charts, 129–130
External markets, 119, 120

## F

Family, 121–132
    erect posture and, 29
    incest, 124
    joint, 122–125
    nuclear/extended, 122
    reciprocity within, 119
    structures, 122–123
Field work, 13–14
Fire, use by early man, 73–74, 152
Fisher, Eugene, 52
Flannery, Kent V., 82
Fossils, 20, 21, 25
    defined, 25
    of man, 25–35
Fried, Morton, 134

## G

Galileo, 5
Genes:
    environment and, 22
    heredity and, 50
Genetic drift, 51
Genotype, 50
Gestures, chimpanzees, 45–46
*Gigantopithecus,* 26
Glaciation (*see* Ice Ages)
Glyphs, 93
Goodall, Jane, 44, 45
Grammar, 63

# H

Hamadryas baboons, 37–38
Hamburg, David A., 154
Hammerstones, 72–73
Hand axes, 73, 74
Harris, Marvin, 20, 106, 111, 114, 135, 140, 151
Hart, C. W. M., 15
Heider, Karl G., 101
Heredity, 22, 49–50
  and intelligence, 57–59
*Homo erectus,* 29–31, 62, 80, 144, 152
  artifacts, 73–75
*Homo sapiens neanderthalensis (see* Neanderthal Man)
*Homo sapiens sapiens (see* Modern man)
Hooton, Ernest, 33
Hostility, 96–97 *(see also* Warfare)
Housing, racism and, 55–56
Human Relations Area Files, 15
Human sacrifice, 151
  Aztecs, 94
Hunting and gathering economies, 113–115
Huxley, Thomas, 1
Hypothesis, 15

# I

Ice Ages, 12, 27, 80, 86
  and sea levels, 27, 80
Ideological subsystem, 110
Ik people, 17
Incest, 124
Indeterminacy, principle of, 6, 72
Individual differences, 21
Individualization, 99–100
Industrialization, 160
Informants, 14
Instinct, vs. learned behavior, 10–11, 97–98
Insulin, discovery of, 10
Intelligence theory, 57–59
Intensification of agriculture, 88–89, 90
Interdependence, lack of, 100
Internal markets, 119–120
Invention, 9–10

Iroquois Indians, 129
Irrigation agriculture, 88, 89, 108, 134

# J

Jensen, Arthur, 57
Joint family, 122–125

# K

Kinship, 128–129
  linking of families, 121, 122, 123–124
  non-familial, 140–141
Kinship charts, 128, 129
Korn, Noel, 31
Krieger, Alex B., 86
Kwakiutl Indians, 117–118

# L

Land:
  collective ownership, 115–116
  private ownership, 116
  scarcity, 133
  value of, 102–104
Language, 9, 10, 31
  change, 64–65
  defined, 62
  diachronic study of, 68
  expansive capacity, 63
  history of, 62
  oral/written, 61, 62, 66–67
  structure of, 61–63
  subcultures, 58
  symbolism of, 65–66
  synchronic study of, 68
Law of evolutionary potential, 159
Law of general evolution, 6–7, 109, 157
Leakey, Louis S. B., 31
Learning, 10
  and instinct, 10–11, 97–98
Legends, 152
  Quetzalcoatl, 93–94, 152
Lewis, Oscar, 140
Linguists, 9
  anthropology and, 67–69

Linnaeus, Carolus, 2, 20
Lowie, 6
Lydell, Charles, 20–21

# M

Man:
    artifacts, 72–84
    brain size, 25, 28–29, 31, 32, 34
    civilization, 85–95
    decalcification, 23, 25, 35, 154
    evolution, 12, 21–35
    fossil evidence, 25–35
    instincts, 98
    race, concept of, 48–60
    reproduction, 22, 24
Manu people, 15, 149
Maori people, 103
Market economies, 118–120
Marriage:
    changing patterns, 130–132
    functions, 121–122
    incest, 124
    linking of families, 121, 122, 123–124
    mate selection, 125, 126–127
    systems, 122–123
    trial, 131
Marshack, Alexander, 78–79
Masai people, 24
Matriarchy, 123
Matrilineage, 123
Matrilocal society, 117, 123
Mayan people, 92–93
Mead, Margaret, 15, 131, 149
Meat-eating:
    baboons, 38
    use of fire and, 74
Melanin, 50
Mendelian populations, 50–51
Mesakin people, 130
Mesolithic period, 80–82
*Mestizo,* 52
Microliths, 80–81
Millon, René F., 92
Mobility, nuclear families and, 125–126
Modern man, 33–35
    artifacts, 77–79
Money, 118–119, 120
Monogamy, 112, 151

Montagu, Ashley, 11
Mormons, 151–152
Morphemes, 63
Morris, Desmond, 47
Munduruccu people, 127
Murphy, Robert F., 127
Mutation, 12, 22, 50
Myths, 152

# N

Nader, Ralph, 142
Natural selection, 21–23, 153
    conservative aspect, 23
Navajo people, 16, 137
Neanderthal Man, 21, 31–33, 62, 80
    artifacts, 75–77
    burial practices, 76, 144–145
Needs:
    aggression, 98
    basic, 12
    satisfaction in baboons, 40–41
Negative entropy, 106
Nelson, Harry, 31
Neolithic period, 9, 80, 82–84
Nuclear family, 122, 125–128
    changing nature, 127–128, 130–132
    kinship chart, 128
Nyakyusa people, 116, 150

# O

Occupational specialization, 90, 117–118
    status ranks, 134–135
Olmec people, 91–92
Oral language, 61, 62

# P

Paleolithic period, 80
Papyrus, 67
*Paranthropus,* 27
Patrilineage, 123
Patrilocal society, 117, 123
Peasant markets, 119
Peking Man, 31

Pelvis, quadruped/biped, 28–29
Pepper moth, 24
Perthes, Boucher de, 20
Phenotype, 50
Phonemes, 62–63
Physical anthropologists, 8
Pictographs, 67
Pilbeam, D. R., 25
Pilling, Arnold R., 15
Pithecanthropus, 21
Plains Indians, 116
Plants, domestication, 82–83, 87, 88, 102, 115
Pleistocene period, 12, 27, 80
Points, 77
Polyandry, 122
Polygamy, 112, 122, 123, 151
Polygyny, 122
Pongidae, 42
Population growth, 25, 115, 133, 154–155
  and ecosystem, 156–159
Populations:
  breeding, 21–23, 29
  Mendelian, 50–51
Ports of trade, 120
Post-Pleistocene period, 80
Potlatch ceremony, 117–118
Pottery:
  archaeological significance, 84
  Mayan, 92–93
  Tehuacán Valley, 87
Poverty, 140–141
Pre-culture, 47
Predation, chimpanzees, 43
Primates, 25
  behavior, 36–47
Principle of indeterminacy, 6, 72
Prosimians, 25
Proto-culture, 47
Puberty rituals, 148
Pueblo Indians, 137
Pygmies:
  Ituri forest, 17, 52
  Oceania, 52
Pyramids, 92, 93

Q

Quetzalcoatl, 93–94, 152

R

Race, 48–60
  biology of, 49–54
  and culture, 49, 53, 58–60
  defined, 49
  social aspect, 48–49, 136
Racism, 49, 136
  in America, 54–60
Rage, vs. warfare, 96–97
Raiding, 100–104
Ramapithecus, 26, 42
Rappaport, Roy, 14
Ray, Vernon, 118
Reciprocity, economy, 114
  within family, 119
Redistribution, 119
  egalitarian/rivalrous, 116
Relative dating, 71
Religion:
  functions, 149–152
  personnel, 146–147
  rituals, 147–149
  and science, 4
Reproduction:
  baboons, 40–41
  chimpanzees, 44
  differing rates, 22, 24
  function of marriage, 121, 123
Reynolds, Frances and Vernon, 44
Rhesus monkeys, social organization, 37
Rites of passage, 148
Rituals:
  birth, 148–149
  group/individual, 147–148
  of intensification, 147–148
  puberty, 148
Rosetta Stone, 67
Ruling groups, 134–135
Rutherford, Ernest, 2

S

Sahlins, Marshal, 109
Sanders, William, 91–92
Schaller, George B., 96
Science:
  concepts of, 2–4
  creativity in, 2–3
  dualistic attitude toward, 1–2

Science (*continued*)
  method, 3–4
  and religion, 4
Security, as function of marriage,
  121, 122, 123
Semai people, 97
Service, Elman, 109, 111, 112, 138
Sexual dimorphism, 27
Shaman, 9, 146
Shanidar Cave, 75–76
Shapiro, Harry, 31
Simons, E. L., 25
Simultaneous discovery, 10
Slash-and-burn agriculture, 108, 115
Slavery, 56, 136, 137
Social organization, 112
  rhesus monkeys, 37
Society:
  classes of, 90, 135
  complexity of modern, 99–100,
    130, 132
  family unit, 121–132
  low- / high-energy, 108–109, 138,
    140, 145
  matrilocal/patrilocal, 117, 123
  organization, 112
  stratified, 117–118, 134–137
Sociopolitical subsystem, 110
Sodalities, 133
Solecki, Ralph, 75, 76
Specialization, occupational, 90, 117–
  118
Species, 49
Spencer, Herbert, 16
Spirits, belief in, 145–146
Star Carr, 81
State structures, 112
  complex society, 157–158
  evolution, 90
  and market economy, 119
Stelae, 91
Stereotypes, 51, 53, 55
Steward, Julian, 110
Stored wealth economies, 117–118
Subcultures, 136–137, 139–140
  black, 58, 136
  Chicano, 136, 137
  defined, 139–140
  Indian, 136–137
  language, 58
  Puerto Rican, 136
Subsistence agriculture, 115–117,
  140

Subsystems, cultural, 110–112
Surplus, 89, 114
Symbolization ability:
  chimpanzees, 46–47
  man, 61–62
Synchronic study, language, 68
Syntax, 62

**T**

Taboo, 124
Taming, vs. domestication, 81
Techno-environmental subsystem,
  110, 113
Technology:
  and cultural selection, 25
  and colonialism, 138
  cumulative nature, 9
  efficiency, 106–109, 133, 156–157
  and environment, 156–159
  and warfare, 104
Tehuacán Valley, 86–88
Tehuantepec, isthmus of, 90–91
*Telandanthropus,* 27
Tenochtitlán, 94–95
Teotihuacán, 85, 92
Terrace agriculture, 88
Territoriality, baboons, 41
Tiwi people, 15
Toltec people, 93–94
Tools, 12, 31
  chimpanzees, 43–44
  fossil man, 72–79
  Mesolithic period, 80–81
Trade, 89, 134
  external markets, 120
Transgenerational culture, 10–11
Trial marriage, 131
Tribe, 6, 108
  defined, 112
Trobriand Islanders, 117
Tsembaga people, 14–15
Tungus, 116
Turnbull, Colin M., 17, 18, 111
Tutankhamen, 85
Tylor, E. B., 1

**U**

Uniformitarianism, 20–21
Usher, Bishop, 20
Utopian communities, 142

# V

Vayda, Andrew, 133
Venuses, 79
Vietnam War, counter-culture and, 142
Villages, 89
  Tehuacán Valley, 87
Violence, 98–100
  in sports, 99
Virchow, Rudolf, 21

# W

Wallace, Alfred, 2, 10
Warfare, 99, 100–104, 133, 158
  Aztecs, 94–95
  vs. rage and hostility, 96–97
  vs. raiding, 100–101
  wars of liberation, 138
Warner, Lloyd, 135

Wheel, invention, 84
White, Leslie, 2, 5, 6, 106, 124
Wilson, Monica, 150
Witches, 149
Written language, 61, 66–67, 93

# X

Xenophobia, 56

# Y

Yahgan people, 11
Yanamamao people, 103

# Z

*Zinjanthropus,* 27